35444002639184
641.5978 JOH
Johns, Amber
Cattlewomen's ranch cookbook

BAR   JUN 0 2 2016

Cattlewomen's RANCH Cookbook

AMBER JOHNS

GIBBS SMITH
TO ENRICH AND INSPIRE HUMANKIND

This book is dedicated to my mom, Barbara, who can make anything into something absolutely delicious.

First Edition
19 18 17 16 15   5 4 3 2 1

Text © 2015 Amber Johns
Photographs © 2015 As noted throughout

All rights reserved. No part of this book may be reproduced by any means whatsoever without written permission from the publisher, except brief portions quoted for purpose of review.

Published by
Gibbs Smith
P.O. Box 667
Layton, Utah 84041

1.800.835.4993 orders
www.gibbs-smith.com

Designed by Kurt Wahlner
Printed and bound in China

Gibbs Smith books are printed on either recycled, 100% post-consumer waste, FSC-certified papers or on paper produced from sustainable PEFC-certified forest/controlled wood source. Learn more at www.pefc.org.

Library of Congress Cataloging-in-Publication Data

Johns, Amber.
  Cattlewomen's ranch cookbook / Amber Johns. — First edition.
     pages cm
  Includes index.
  ISBN 978-1-4236-3701-1
  1. Cooking, American—Western style. I. Title.
  TX715.2.W47J64 2015
  641.5978—dc23
                            2014034367

Contents

Introduction 6
Ranch Cooking 9
Cooking on the Range 11
Breakfasts 13
Breads 27
Appetizers 37
Soups, Stews, and Salads 45
Side Dishes 67
Main Dishes 83
Desserts 125
This and That 157
About the Author 171
Index 172

Introduction

In a ranch or farm kitchen right now a cattlewoman is cooking. It might be a new recipe or it might be one she made with her grandmother and has used through the years. No matter, new or old, she takes pride in the ingredients—for she has raised the livestock and tended to the gardens year after year. This recipe will definitely be passed on with pride to the next generation.

The CattleWomen's organization is a group of women who formed an association in the mid-1900s. This group of women shared the same vision—to promote the ranching industry and support the Cattlemen's Association. Formerly known as the CowBelles, these ladies have expanded the vision of their organization and have become a stronger voice, not only in the ranching industry, but in the farming industry as well. The CattleWomen, as their group is known today, are very instrumental in the promotion, awareness, and education of the ranching and farming industries. It is not necessary to live on a ranch, a farm, or even own a cow to become a member of the CattleWomen's organization. They welcome anyone who is passionate about the ranching and farming industries. These ladies keep up on the latest news and political agendas affecting the industries they promote by attending local and regional meetings and conferences. They are instrumental in educating the people in their communities concerning beef cuts, proper meat handling, beef by-products, and stewardship practices. They raise money for scholarships for local youth, organize beef recipe demonstrations at the local grocery stores, participate in ranch tours, and donate beef for Father's Day and to senior citizen centers. This is just a short list of the outreach programs that CattleWomen chapters across the country perform within their communities.

They stay on top of the latest food trends and create recipes that will fit every lifestyle. However, they have still not forgotten those timeless, tried-and-true recipes of their grandmothers and great-grandmothers. These recipes that have been passed down from generation to generation are still used today and are family favorites. The *Cattlewomen's Ranch Cookbook* contains old and new recipes from CattleWomen across the country who so graciously and willingly shared their legacy that reaches back into the deepest roots of America's history, the ranching and farming industries.

Ranch Cooking

How it was and how it is

Ranch cooking has always been delicious, but how the cooking is done has changed a bit over the years. In the early days, cooking was a task and the ingredients were simple. The food was homegrown. The meat was butchered at the ranch, milk was fresh from the cow, butter was made in the crock, eggs were taken from the chicken coop, and the vegetables were picked from the garden outback. Everything needed to create a satisfying, nutritious meal was outside. The food on the ranchers' tables was their own. Families worked hard to manage, grow, and raise what was on their table. Sugar and flour came in 50 and 100 pound sacks, respectively, that was picked up from town the previous month. Simple ingredients turned into delicious meals.

Everything was eaten or made into something. Food was not wasted. Vegetables and fruit were canned and was meat cured to make it through the winter. Bread was made on a daily basis if ingredients were available. The women cooked three big meals a day—breakfast, lunch, and dinner. The typical meals for one day, 100 years ago, would have looked something like

Photo courtesy of Amber Johns.

the following: Breakfast—oatmeal and heavy cream, breakfast beefsteak with creamed potatoes, buckwheat cakes, bacon, hot syrup and melted butter, apple pandowdy with sweet cream, tea, and coffee. Lunch or the noon meal—green pea soup with diced salt pork, boiled ham and egg sauce, potato croquettes, escalloped tomatoes, homemade bread and freshly churned butter, coleslaw, sweet 'n' sour pickles, pudding, and pie. Dinner or the evening meal—creamed chicken and biscuits, cold sliced ham, baked potatoes, succotash, pickles, spiced peaches, cake, and ice cream*. The work was grueling from sun up to sun down and the crew always hungry. Everyone had a hand in the ranch work from the youngest to the oldest. It took them all to survive.

Today, some of the challenges we face as cooks are questions such as what type of milk do we buy, organic or non-organic? Turkey or beef? White or wheat or whole-grain bread? And we wonder, "Is real butter bad for us?" Our meat is not hanging in the shed outback, but is nicely wrapped in the freezer, labeled to tell us what it is. If we are lucky, it will have a sticker labeling it grown and raised in the USA. And, if the sticker isn't there, we really do not have not a clue as to where that meat came from. The milk is in a plastic jug, the eggs are in a carton, and the butter is in tubs or sticks. Our sugar and flour are nicely put away in decorative containers out on the counter. There is no fear of dinner being our last meal. There is no fear of not having enough food to make it through the winter. We have the luxury of grocery stores within a short drive from our homes.

With the invention of refrigeration, motorized vehicles, and grocery stores, cooking isn't the chore it used to be. Our recipes today have evolved with technology. They are simple, fast, and delicious, making cooking an enjoyable quick task, rather than an all-day job.

---

*Information taken from the cookbook, *Reflections, Bicentennial-Centennial*, 1976 *Reflections Cookbook*, Custer County, Colorado.

Cooking on the Range

As a kid, I lived on my family's commercial Hereford ranch on the California-Oregon border long enough to get me hooked on the ranching life. Today, I live with my husband and toddler daughter on the Alvord Ranch in Eastern Oregon, 120 miles from the nearest town with a grocery store. We may not be able to see movies when they first come out in theaters or afford a week-long European vacation, but when I eat grilled steak with mushrooms and sautéed asparagus at home I can't help but think, "This is the good life."

Before marriage, I was on the cowboy crew, so I know how exhausted those guys are after a ten-hour day of gathering yearlings off the desert with no food or water. It's beyond refreshing for the body and soul to turn out your horse and sit down at the table to a plateful of steaming hot beef in tomato sauce over rice and a cold glass of lemonade. Now, I love being able to provide that comfort for others on the ranch.

Since I'm now a mom and can no longer doctor calves or move cattle all day with the cowboy crew, I have learned to find adventures in the kitchen by trying new recipes. My transition from full-time cowboy to full-time homemaker wasn't as smooth as turkey gravy, however. I was initially overwhelmed with my new role as family's head cook/dishwasher/food-cleaner-upper-off-the-floor. It was an unpleasant shock to realize these people expected to eat every day, and that this would require me to take inventory of our fridge and cupboards, purchase food, heat, chill or prepare it as necessary, wash the dishes, and do it all again the following day. It was a relentless cycle with few interludes as a remote ranch wife can't drive to a restaurant once a week to take a break from cooking and dish washing. I realized if I wanted to eat good food, I had to learn to cook it myself.

Cooking on a remote ranch is a little different than cooking in town, and by "a little" I mean "totally, completely different with few, if any, similarities beyond a hot stove and a countertop." I grocery shop once a month, which means I run out of fresh produce after about ten days. Most of my dishes end up being "with a twist" because I don't have all the proper ingredients. I operate on a 75 percent rule: if I have 75 percent of the listed ingredients for a new recipe, I'll give it a try. I also buy cheese by the six-pound block and always keep bacon in the freezer. When we're low on groceries, these can go a long way in producing edible, even tasty, food for our table. No one has ever said, "Man, I wish you hadn't put bacon/cheese on that."

A cowman I worked for when I was dating my husband told me that when he and his wife married, they scraped by on cowboy wages. They agreed to not skimp on groceries, as having good food can ease the strain of other shortcomings in material possessions. My husband and I agreed to follow this policy as well. The cowman also told me that when fighting with my spouse, we should always fight naked. My husband voted to eagerly embrace this gem of marital advice, but his wife is not yet convinced. I am convinced, though, that a (mostly) healthy diet of various delicious foods helps create a welcoming atmosphere in the home, and so I strive to learn new recipes. I haven't seen a new release in the theater in years, and I may never see the Riviera, but between the pumpkin chocolate chip cookies, homemade bread, and high-desert scenery, I am definitely living the good life.

—Jolyn Young

Sourdough Hotcakes

Serves 2–4

BETH ANDERSON
WILLOW SPRINGS RANCH
CALLAO, UTAH

The "hot griddle" we use is a cast iron furnace bottom that my dad, David C. Bagley, got out of the old CCC barracks that he bought to change into a home. We would feed hundreds of people sourdough hotcakes, bacon, and eggs when they would come to tour the Willow Springs Overland Stage/Pony Express Station at our ranch. It is the only privately owned station still in use on the trail.

Starter

2 cups flour
2 cups warm water
1 package dry yeast (1 1/4 teaspoons)

Hotcakes

2 eggs
1 teaspoon baking soda
1 teaspoon salt
1 tablespoon sugar
3 tablespoons sweet or sour cream (or melted fat)

Starter: Mix flour, water, and yeast together and let set until yeast starts to get bubbly. Set aside 1/4 cup starter for next time.

Hotcakes: Beat eggs, baking soda, salt, and sugar with fork and blend in starter. Add cream and mix well. I usually mix in the entire starter and make a fresh one the night before I want hotcakes for breakfast. Bake on a hot griddle. Turn once. The bubbles that form will pop when it is ready to turn. This recipe is easily multiplied to feed lots of folks.

BAGLEY RANCH 109 YEARS
WILLOW SPRINGS RANCH
20 YEARS CALLAO, UTAH

Photos courtesy of the Anderson family.

My great-grandpa Charles Stuart Bagley purchased the Overland Stage/Pony Express Station at Willow Springs in 1886 with 160 acres. I am the fifth generation to be here on the ranch. After we moved back to the ranch, we decided to call it Willow Springs after the station that still stands. My great-grandpa came for a place to run his horses. He furnished many horses for the Spanish-American War. The last time they branded, they had over 90 colts after 1908. We are now a commercial cow/calf operation, raising hay for the cattle on the natural meadows and fields that provided hay and water for the "home" station in the early stage and Pony Express days. We have the largest Fremont Cottonwood Tree in the state of Utah and second largest in the nation.

My father David C. Bagley was one of the first ranchers to keep records and track tenderness on beef cattle. He showed that the crossbreds were better than the purebred Herefords they started with. He crossed the Herefords with Simmentals using a full artificial insemination (AI) program. My husband Don convinced me that we could make more money going to all black cattle. We are now ninety-five percent black with crosses in Black Angus, Black Ghelvieh, and Black Simmental. We have been able to keep the good genetic traits as two of our children have won the county carcass contest at the local fair.

Bill's Coffee Cake

Serves 4–6

GERRI VAN NORMAN
REED STATION
TUSCARORA, NEVADA

Topping

- 1/4 cup brown sugar
- 1 tablespoon flour
- 1 teaspoon cinnamon
- 1 tablespoon melted butter
- 1/2 cup chopped nuts, of choice

Cake

- 1/4 cup canola oil
- 1 egg, beaten
- 1/2 cup milk
- 1 1/2 cups sifted flour
- 3/4 cup sugar
- 2 teaspoons baking powder
- 1/2 teaspoon salt

Topping: Combine the brown sugar, flour, cinnamon, and butter. Add the nuts and stir to incorporate.

Cake: Preheat oven to 375 degrees and grease a 9 x 9-inch pan.

Combine the oil, egg, and milk in a large bowl. Mix together the dry ingredients then add to milk mixture. Mix well.

Pour batter into the prepared pan. Sprinkle with topping then bake for 25 minutes.

Breakfast Casserole

Serves 6–8

BONNIE GASPARD
MAURICE, LOUISIANA

2 cans refrigerated crescent rolls
1 (16-ounce) package Jimmy Dean breakfast sausage (I use the HOT)
1 (4.5-ounce) can chopped green chiles
1 (8-ounce) block cream cheese
12 eggs lightly scrambled (do not fully cook)

Preheat oven to 350 degrees and grease a 9 x 13-inch baking dish. You can use nonstick cooking spray.

Layer 1 can of crescent rolls on the bottom of the prepared baking dish. Just roll out right from the can. If pastry pulls apart while doing this, pinch back together. Bake this for about 5 minutes to prevent sogginess.

In a skillet, brown the sausage. When sausage is fully cooked, add the green chiles and cream cheese to sausage. Stir to combine and melt the cheese. Put sausage mixture on top of the bottom layer of crescent rolls. Layer on the eggs. Layer the other can of crescent rolls on top of mixture just as done for the bottom layer. Bake according to time on crescent roll cans, approximately 12–15 minutes.

German Pancakes

Serves 4–6

**RACHEL BUZZETTI
LAMOILLE, NEVADA**

½ stick butter
6 eggs
1 cup milk
1 cup flour
¼ teaspoon salt
Powdered sugar

Preheat oven to 400 degrees. Melt butter in bottom of an 8 x 8-inch pan.

Mix eggs, milk, flour, and salt together; pour into pan. Bake for 20 minutes. Sprinkle with powdered sugar and serve warm.

Pancakes and Eggs 'n' Hamburger Breakfast

Serves 4–6

MOLLY WOLF
WOLF AND SONS RANCHES
NORTH FORK, NEVADA

Pancakes

> 1 cup milk
> 1 cup flour
> 2 teaspoons baking powder
> 1/4 teaspoon salt
> 1/4 cup vegetable oil
> 3 eggs

Combine milk, flour, baking powder, salt, oil, and eggs together and let rest while heating griddle. Cook pancakes on a hot griddle until golden brown on each side.

Eggs 'n' Hamburger

> 1 pound ground beef
> Salt and pepper, to taste
> Seasoned salt, to taste
> 4 eggs

Brown the ground beef and season with salt, pepper, and seasoned salt. Then crack the eggs into mixture. Stir eggs into ground beef and cook until eggs are done. Serve with the pancakes.

Photos courtesy of the Wolf family.

Oven-Baked French Toast

Serves 8–10

DEBRA COCKRELL
COCKRELL RANCHES & LODGING
CEDARVILLE, CALIFORNIA
WWW.HIGHDESERTLODGING.COM

This is a great recipe for those 4:00 AM breakfasts before going out and gathering cattle. It is something you can prepare the night before if you want.

Syrup

    2 cups brown sugar
    2 sticks butter
    1/3 cup corn syrup

French Toast

    12 eggs
    2 1/2 cups milk
    1 tablespoon vanilla
    2 loaves French bread, sliced, or thick deli-sliced bread
    Sprinkle of cinnamon
    1(8-ounce) block cream cheese cut into small cubes, optional

Syrup: Melt brown sugar, butter, and corn syrup over low heat.

French Toast: Preheat oven to 325 degrees prior to baking. Prepare a large baking sheet with sides or a large deep-dish cake pan with nonstick cooking spray. Pour syrup mixture into bottom of pan.

Beat eggs, milk, and vanilla together. Arrange bread over syrup mixture, pour egg mixture over bread using as much as will fit. Sprinkle with cinnamon. Cover with aluminum foil and refrigerate overnight, or leave uncovered and bake right away. If using the next morning, uncover before cooking. Bake for 30 minutes. Right before it is done, place cream cheese cubes over the top and let melt in oven or spread over top when soft. Serve from the baking pan. This recipe goes well with breakfast meat and fruit.

COCKRELL RANCHES
CEDARVILLE, CALIFORNIA

This ranching family has been dedicated to the cattle and ranching industry for a span of six generations. Their ancestors were early settlers in the Surprise Valley area. Their love for ranching and for the area has stayed with the family throughout all the generations while running cattle in Northeastern California and Western Nevada.

It was a very common site over the years to see the Cockrells trailing the cattle home over the dusty trails and roads from their Nevada range. All of the kids made the ride in front of the saddle of Will and Deb, or starting on their own at the age of three, perched upon a trusty horse for that twenty-eight mile trail drive home. The long line of cattle stretched down Main Street of Cedarville.

Photos courtesy of the Cockrell family.

Chocolate Chip-Banana Pancakes

Serves 4–6

RACHEL PARKER
PARKER RANCHES
IBAPAH, UTAH

I am a beginning rancher (I married a rancher) and was in need of finding something my kids would eat at breakfast besides cold cereal. My kids love bananas and chocolate, so these ended up in the pancakes one day. It is just one of our favorite recipes. My family loves to eat this no matter what meal it is served for.

1 1/4 cups flour
1 tablespoon sugar
2 teaspoons baking powder
1/2 teaspoon salt
1/2 teaspoon cinnamon
1 1/4 cups milk
1 small ripe banana, mashed (about 1/2 cup)
1 large egg
1 teaspoon vanilla
1/3 cup semisweet chocolate mini morsels, divided

Combine flour, sugar, baking powder, salt, and cinnamon in a large bowl. After mixing well, stir in the milk, banana, egg, and vanilla. Fold in 1/4 cup chocolate morsels. Pour batter onto a heated griddle, making 3-inch rounds. Flip and serve with remaining morsels sprinkled on top of pancakes.

Whole-Wheat Waffles

Serves 4–6

**GINGER JOHNSON
AURORA, UTAH**

2 eggs, separated
1 cup whole-wheat flour
1 tablespoon baking soda
1/2 teaspoon salt
2 teaspoons sugar
1 1/4 cups milk
1/2 cup vegetable oil (can substitute 1/4 cup applesauce and 1/4 cup oil)

In a small bowl, beat egg whites until fluffy and set aside. In a large bowl, beat egg yolks, dry ingredients, and milk, and then add oil and beat 2 minutes. Fold in egg whites. Cook batter in a heated waffle iron. These freeze well and then you can toast in your toaster for a quick breakfast.

COWGIRLS AT THE TRIANGLE RANCH RODEO. (DOUBLEDAY)

Breads

Coconut Zucchini Bread

Makes 2 loaves

SHERRY SPENCER
SPENCER LAND & LIVESTOCK
YOST, UTAH

3 eggs, beaten
1 1/2 cups sugar
1 cup vegetable oil
1 cup chopped nuts, of choice, optional
3 cups grated zucchini
1 1/2 cups shredded coconut
1 teaspoon coconut extract
2 teaspoons vanilla
3 cups flour
1 teaspoon baking soda
1 teaspoon salt
1 teaspoon baking powder

Preheat oven to 325 degrees and grease 2 loaf pans.
Mix together the eggs, sugar, and oil in a large bowl. Add the rest of the ingredients in order listed. Mix well. Pour into prepared pans and bake for 1 hour. Let cool in the pans for 15 minutes before turning out onto cooling racks.

French Bread

Makes 2 loaves

BILLIE SUE SLAGOWSKI
SLAGOWSKI RANCHES, INC.
PINE VALLEY, NEVADA

This recipe came to me from my mother-in-law, Charlene Slagowski. Charlene was a phenomenal cook. She was known for amazing pies and her handmade cards.

 1 cup boiling water
 1 tablespoon sugar
 1 tablespoon salt
 1 tablespoon shortening
 1 cup cold water
 1 package yeast, dissolved in $1/4$ cup warm water
 $4 1/2$ to 5 cups flour
 1 egg white, slightly beaten

Place the boiling water in a large bowl and stir in the sugar, salt, and shortening to dissolve. Add cold water. Allow to cool. Add the yeast when water mixture has cooled to warm and set aside until the yeast bubbles.

Mix in 1 cup of flour at a time. Add just enough flour that when you touch the dough it leaves a slight indent and doesn't stick to your finger. I have found that less flour will make better bread. Knead lightly—I use the dough hook on my mixer and don't knead.

Shape your loaves on a greased baking sheet and brush with egg white. Slash loaves at a diagonal before rising. Let rise until double in size.

Preheat oven to 350 degrees and then bake for 35–40 minutes or until nicely browned.

Homemade Bread

Makes 2 loaves

CLAUDETTE BROUSSARD
VERMILION PARISH CATTLEWOMEN
ABBEVILLE, LOUISIANA
COLUMBUS PLANTATION

This recipe has been in my family for years. As a young 4-H member I used this for a demonstration. It is very easy to make.

- 2 packages yeast
- 1 1/4 cups warm water
- 2 tablespoons sugar
- 4 tablespoons cooking oil
- 1 teaspoon salt
- 4 to 4 1/2 cups flour

Dissolve yeast in warm water. Add sugar, oil, and salt and mix well. Add flour, 1 cup at a time, and knead until dough is elastic and shiny.

Place in a large greased bowl, cover, and let rise 45 minutes.

Shape dough into 2 rounds and place in greased loaf pans. Let rise 30 minutes.

Preheat oven to 350 degrees and bake for 45–60 minutes.

Mexican Cornbread

Serves 8–10

BONNIE GASPARD
MAURICE, LOUISIANA

3 eggs
3 cups grated cheddar cheese
1/2 cup vegetable oil
1 (15-ounce) can whole corn with liquid
1 (15-ounce) can creamed corn
1 teaspoon garlic powder
1 cup evaporated milk
1 large onion, finely chopped
1 cup chopped jalapeño peppers
2 cups packaged cornbread mix
1 to 2 smoked sausages, cut into bite-size pieces
1 teaspoon salt

Preheat oven to 400 degrees and prepare a 9 x 13-inch pan with nonstick cooking spray. Mix everything together in a large bowl. Pour into prepared pan and bake for 45 minutes.

Photo courtesy of Lou Basanez.

Ham and Cheese Muffins

Serves 12

LOU BASANEZ
MOUNTAIN CITY, NEVADA

1/2 cup milk
3 tablespoons vegetable oil
1 egg
3/4 cup grated cheddar cheese
1/2 cup diced ham
1/2 cup chopped green bell pepper
1/2 cup chopped onion

Preheat oven to 425 degrees and grease cups of a 12-cup muffin tin.
Slightly beat milk, oil, and egg in a large bowl. Stir in the remaining ingredients with fork until moistened.
Divide evenly among cups in the muffin tin. Bake for 15–20 minutes.

Peach Muffins

Serves 12

**RACHEL BUZZETTI
LAMOILLE, NEVADA**

> 1/2 cup butter or margarine
> 3/4 cup sugar
> 1 egg
> 1/2 cup plain yogurt or sour cream
> 1 teaspoon vanilla
> 1 1/2 cups flour
> 1 1/2 teaspoons baking powder
> 1 cup chopped fresh, frozen, or canned peaches, well drained
> 1 cup chopped pecans

Preheat oven to 400 degrees and grease cups of a 12-cup muffin tin.

Cream butter and sugar together in a large bowl. Add egg, yogurt, and vanilla; beat well. Combine flour and baking powder in a separate bowl and add to first mixture. Fold in peaches and pecans.

Divide evenly among cups in the muffin tin. Bake for 20 minutes.

Pumpkin Muffins

Makes 24 muffins

MOLLY WOLF
WOLF AND SONS RANCHES
NORTH FORK, NEVADA

This recipe came from my nephew. He made these in his preschool class and it has been a favorite breakfast muffin for him since.

5 eggs
1 1/4 cups canola oil
1 (15-ounce) can pumpkin pie mix (Libby's)
2 cups flour
2 cups sugar
2 small packages cook and serve vanilla pudding
1 teaspoon baking powder
1 teaspoon cinnamon
1/2 teaspoon pumpkin spice
1/2 teaspoon salt

Preheat oven to 325 degrees and grease or prepare with paper liners 2 (12-cup) muffin tins.
Mix all ingredients together in a large bowl. Divide evenly among the muffin cups and bake for 20–22 minutes.

Photo courtesy of Amber Johns.

Appetizers

Corn Dip

Serves 8–10

BONNIE GASPARD
MAURICE, LOUISIANA

2 (15–ounce) cans whole-kernel corn
1 (10-ounce) can Rotel tomatoes
1 cup diced jalapeño peppers
8 ounces sour cream
8 ounces mayonnaise
1 bunch green onions, chopped
1 tablespoon Accent seasoning
1 tablespoon garlic powder
12 ounces grated cheddar cheese
Chips or crackers, of choice

Mix everything together, except chips, and place into a serving bowl. This dip is good cold or warmed. Serve with chips or crackers.

Easy Ranch Appetizer

Serves 8–10

MOLLY WOLF
WOLF AND SONS RANCHES
NORTH FORK, NEVADA

> 1 (8-ounce) block cream cheese
> 1 (8- to 10-ounce) jar of jalapeño jelly, preferably homemade
> Crackers, of choice

Place the cream cheese in the middle of a serving dish. Spoon a generous amount of the jelly over the cream cheese. You may not need the whole jar. Serve with crackers and enjoy.

★★★★★★★★★★★★★★★★★★★★★★★★★★★★★★★★★★★★★

Pecan Dip

Serving size depends on how much you would like to make

BONNIE GASPARD
MAURICE, LOUISIANA

> Equal parts of each ingredient
>   Grated cheddar cheese
>   Mayonnaise
>   Chopped pecans
>   Chopped green onion tops
>   Pepper jelly
>   Crackers or corn chips

Mix cheese, mayonnaise, pecans, and onion together and serve with pepper jelly on top. Use as a dip for crackers or corn chips.

Surprise Meatballs

Serves 8

**JULIE GUBLER
GUBLER RANCH LLC
SANTA CLARA, UTAH**

This recipe makes a great appetizer as well as a main dish. The sauce is tasty with rice, and the whole recipe freezes well.

Meatballs

6 mozzarella cheese sticks
2 pounds ground beef
1 cup bread crumbs
1/4 cup milk
1 egg
1/2 cup minced onion
1 clove garlic, minced
1 teaspoon salt
1/4 teaspoon pepper

Sauce

1 cup ketchup
1/2 cup Worcestershire sauce
1/2 cup cider vinegar
1/2 cup brown sugar
1 clove garlic, minced
1 tablespoon minced onion

Preheat oven to 500 degrees.
Cut cheese sticks into 8 cubes per stick for a total of 48 cubes. Freeze the cheese cubes for a few minutes until ready to use.

Combine the rest of the meatball ingredients until well mixed. Take the cheese cubes from the freezer and wrap about 2 tablespoons of meatball mixture around each cheese cube. Seal so there is no cheese showing. Place meatballs close together in a 9 x 13-inch pan. Bake for 15 minutes.

Meanwhile, combine sauce ingredients. Reduce oven heat to 350 degrees. Pour sauce over meatballs and cook for another 10–15 minutes until sauce is heated.

GUBLER RANCH LLC
SANTA CLARA, UTAH   711

Ranching has been in the Gubler family for several generations. Our ranches have extended from Central Utah to Nevada to the Arizona Strip. The current ranch was started by Dale Gubler and passed down to his son, Bill, along with the 711 brand which is an Arizona Strip brand.

Val's Salsa

Serves 6–8

KARI JOHNSON
JOHNSON LAND AND LIVESTOCK
RUSH VALLEY, UTAH

1 (15-ounce) can black beans, rinsed and drained
1 (11-ounce) can white shoepeg corn, drained
2 to 3 Roma tomatoes, diced
Fresh or dried cilantro, to taste
Dried red onion or green onion, to taste
2 avocados, diced
2 cloves garlic, minced
1/2 cup Italian dressing
Chips

Mix all ingredients, except chips, together and serve with chips.

Soups, Stews, and Salads

Corn and Squash Soup

Serves 6–8

**GINGER JOHNSON
AURORA, UTAH**

2 plus cups grated crookneck squash
2 to 3 corn cobs, kernels cut off the cob (substitute frozen corn)
2 cups grated carrots
2 1/2 cups water
2 small onions, chopped
1 green bell pepper, chopped
1 tablespoon butter
1/3 cup flour, more if needed
3 1/2 to 5 cups milk, to taste
Garlic powder, to taste
Salt and pepper, to taste
Crumbled bacon
Grated cheddar cheese

Bring squash, corn, carrots, and water to a boil in a large saucepan and simmer until tender.

Saute the onions, bell pepper, and butter in a stockpot then add the flour and milk. Season with garlic powder and salt and pepper. Stir continuously until thickened and then add cooked vegetables. Garnish each serving with bacon and cheese.

Good Brown Stew

Serves 10–12

DOROTHY CHESSER
HOLMAN, TEXAS
TEXAS COASTAL CATTLEWOMEN

    2 pounds stew meat, cut into 1-inch cubes and browned
    2 cups hot water
    2 small bay leaves
    1 teaspoon lemon juice
    2 teaspoons salt
    1 teaspoon Worcestershire sauce
    $1/2$ teaspoon pepper
    1 clove garlic, minced
    Pinch of allspice
    6 carrots, halved
    3 or 4 potatoes, quartered
    3 onions, chopped

Add meat, water, bay leaves, lemon juice, salt, Worcestershire sauce, pepper, garlic, and allspice to a pressure cooker and pressure cook for 20 minutes or cook in a large skillet on top of the stove until the meat is tender.

Open cooker and add carrots, potatoes, and onions; remove bay leaves. If using a skillet, add vegetables and cover.

Continue cooking vegetables until done. Remove meat and vegetables and thicken liquid. (I use 3 tablespoons of quick-cooking tapioca to thicken the liquid). Return meat and vegetables to liquid for a great stew.

PYBURN RANCH

My sister and I have a ranch in Holman, Texas; it is located near Weimar, Texas, in the Hill Country. We inherited the ranch from our parents, who purchased it in 1953. The ranch is located on the Colorado River, so we have been fortunate to have had a source of water during the drought in Texas. We have Hereford cows bred to Brahman bulls and mix-breed cows on Charolaise bulls. We also have native pecans, which is extra income.

There are white-tail deer on the ranch and we enjoy hunting. Two stock tanks and the river make a nice place to fish.

There are three houses on the ranch. One is for my sister, one is for me, and the other we call the Grandchildren's Place. Along with the houses comes three yards to mow.

Barbara Smith's Chili

Serves 6–8

BETTY GARNER
CRYSTAL ACRES FARM
DANVILLE, ARKANSAS

This chili recipe came from a family friend who made up the recipe herself. We love chili, but do not like it too spicy. This recipe is a favorite at church dinners.

- 1 pound ground beef or deer
- 1 large onion, chopped
- 1 green bell pepper, chopped
- 1 teaspoon minced garlic
- 1 (16-ounce) can stewed tomatoes
- 1 (16-ounce) can Rotel tomatoes
- 1 tablespoon chili seasoning mix
- 1 tablespoon chili powder
- 1/4 cup brown sugar

Brown meat with onion, bell pepper, and garlic in a large saucepan. Pour off any grease.

Add remaining ingredients. Simmer for 30 minutes or longer. If you need more liquid, add a beef bouillon cube and water. The longer you simmer the chili, the better it is. Taste and add additional seasoning if you want it spicier.

Easy Beef and Black Bean Chili

Serves 10–12

ED AND DEANA ALDER
HALE HOMESTEAD
TROUT CREEK, UTAH

1 tablespoon olive oil
1 medium yellow onion, diced
1 tablespoon chopped garlic
1 (32-ounce) can crushed tomatoes
1/2 pound leftover pot roast, cubed
1 (15-ounce) can black beans, drained
1 1/2 tablespoons chili powder
2 cups water
Salt and freshly ground black pepper, to taste
1/4 cup grated Monterey Jack cheese

Heat a large saucepan over medium heat and add the oil, onion, and garlic; saute until the onion is golden, about 5 minutes. Add the tomatoes, pot roast, black beans, chili powder, and water. Lower the heat and simmer for 30 minutes. Season with salt and pepper. Ladle the chili into serving bowls and sprinkle each bowl with 1 tablespoon cheese. Serve hot.

HALE HOMESTEAD
ED AND DEANA ALDER
TROUT CREEK, UTAH

The Hale Homestead started by a filing for a homestead by two brothers, Nathan L. Hale and his older brother Ivan in 1938. Drilled wells provided water through a natural flowing artesian system that ponded enough water daily to flood irrigate. In 1972, electric power was introduced to the entire Snake Valley which allowed a more dependable and adequate water source.

Photo courtesy of the Alder family.

Ed and Deana Alder purchased the homestead in 1992 where they raised six children through the age of majority. They have nineteen grandchildren and currently chase fifty mother cows.

As one-cylinder diesel power plants and kerosene oil lamps were stored in forgotten corners of sheds, the introduction of phone lines in 1984, the access and growth of the internet, and the culture of dish networks and Facebook rocketed this area into the modern world.

The reality of living in this unique, wonderful, beautiful part of the world is that the nearest asphalt road is fifty miles away, hospital and doctor services are 100 miles away, and store and gas station conveniences are sixty miles depending on the road taken. When the sunsets amaze, the desert rain storms humble, and the silence is deafening, the Alders know that they made the best decision of where to live and raise their family.

Cauliflower Broccoli Salad

Serves 8–10

ROBIN LUFKIN
LUFKIN CATTLE COMPANY
LEMHI, IDAHO

3 cups broccoli florets
3 cups cauliflower florets
1/2 cup cashew pieces
1/2 cup craisins
1 pound bacon, fried and crumbled

Dressing

1 cup mayonnaise
1/2 cup white sugar
6 tablespoons red wine vinegar

Combine the broccoli and cauliflower in a large bowl. Add the cashews and Craisins, and then stir in the bacon.
Stir the dressing ingredients together and pour over the vegetable mixture. Refrigerate for several hours or overnight before serving. Stir often to help incorporate ingredients together.

Mom's Simple Coleslaw

Serves 6–8

MOLLY WOLF
WOLF AND SONS RANCHES
NORTH FORK, NEVADA

My mother-in-law is known for not following recipes. This is one of her recipes that she created. It is an excellent accompaniment to barbecue ribs.

1 (13-ounce) jar Lighthouse Ranch Dressing
Milk, to taste
Sugar, to taste
Salt and pepper, to taste
1 (16-ounce) package coleslaw

Mix dressing with milk, sugar, salt, and pepper until desired flavor and consistency. Toss with coleslaw.

Variations: This recipe also has some variations. You can use 1 bottle of Lighthouse Sweet or Zesty Italian Dressing for a whole different coleslaw. You can add a little wow to the recipe by adding in chopped apples, pecans, or more grated carrots.

Coleslaw

Serves 6–8

**JAMIE JO AXTELL
AXTELL CATTLE COMPANY
ANTON, COLORADO**

This recipe was handed down from my husband's side of the family. This is his Aunt Bonnie's recipe.

Dressing

1/2 cup mayonnaise or Miracle Whip
3/4 teaspoon salt
Dash of pepper
Dash of paprika
1/2 teaspoon sugar
1 tablespoon vinegar
1 tablespoon milk

Salad

3 to 4 cups chopped cabbage
1/4 cup diced green bell pepper
1 teaspoon salt
1/4 teaspoon pepper
1/2 teaspoon dry mustard
1 teaspoon celery seeds
2 tablespoons sugar
1 tablespoon diced pimientos
1 teaspoon grated onion

Mix together dressing ingredients and refrigerate. Toss together salad ingredients, cover, and refrigerate until cabbage wilts (4–12 hours). Drain off excess liquid, add dressing, and serve.

Country Pea Salad

Serves 12–14

RACHEL BUZZETTI
LAMOILLE, NEVADA

    2 (16-ounce) cans peas, drained
    2 tablespoons minced onion
    1/4 cup finely diced celery
    1/2 cup cubes cheddar cheese
    2 hard-boiled eggs
    1/4 teaspoon salt
    1/8 teaspoon pepper
    1/2 cup mayonnaise

Combine peas, onion, celery, and cheese in a large bowl. Chop eggs; add to salad mixture. Season with salt and pepper and add mayonnaise; lightly toss and serve.

Deb's Beefy Pasta Salad

Serves 12–14

DEBRA COCKRELL
COCKRELL RANCHES & LODGING
CEDARVILLE, CALIFORNIA

Our ranch is big on using tri-tip in many ways. This recipe is one easy way to take it along whether you are riding the range or taking it to a neighbor's branding. I use it with or without beef. It makes for a great balanced meal all by itself. Add or subtract anything you like. This is a great recipe for big crowds or brandings.

1 beef tri-tip
Montreal Seasoning, to taste
2 (16-ounce) boxes Ronzoni Penne Rigate pasta
3 (3.5-ounce) cans sliced black olives
1 (15-ounce) can garbanzo beans, rinsed and drained
1 (15-ounce) can kidney beans, rinsed and drained
1 (10-ounce) can black beans, rinsed and drained
$1/2$ cup crumbled feta cheese
1 cup chopped fresh spinach
$1/2$ cup chopped red onion
$1/2$ cup sunflower seeds
1 teaspoon fennel seeds
$1/2$ cup grated or matchstick carrot
1 head fresh broccoli crowns, chopped

Dressing

1 1/2 cups vegetable oil
1/3 cup balsamic vinegar
1 packet Good Seasons Cheese & Garlic Dressing mix
1 teaspoon sesame seeds
1/4 cup orange marmalade jam

Rub the meat with Montreal Seasoning and let marinate for 1 hour. Barbecue the tri-tip to desired doneness. Let set and completely cool. Slice the beef then slice again into thin strips.

Cook pasta according package directions; drain. Place pasta into a big bowl. Add all other ingredients and combine. Toss with dressing a half hour before serving.

Dressing: Place all ingredients into a jar and shake well before adding to pasta salad. Best if made several hours before using. Or, use other dressing of choice.

Photo collage by Debra Cockrell, Cedarville, California.

Frog-Eye Salad

Serves 14–16

MOLLY WOLF
WOLF AND SONS RANCHES
NORTH FORK, NEVADA

1 (16-ounce) package acini di pepe pasta
2 1/2 teaspoons salt, divided
1 teaspoon olive oil
1 cup sugar
1/2 teaspoon salt
2 tablespoons flour
2 eggs, beaten
1 3/4 cups pineapple juice
1 tablespoon lemon juice
2 (16-ounce) cans Mandarin oranges, drained
2 (20-ounce) cans pineapple tidbits or crushed, drained
2 cups mini marshmallows
1 cup shredded coconut
2 (9-ounce) containers whipped topping

Boil pasta according to package directions, adding 2 teaspoons salt and olive oil; rinse and cool. Place in a large bowl.
Cook sugar, remaining salt, flour, eggs, and juices in a saucepan until thickened. Add sauce to the pasta. Stir the oranges, pineapple, and marshmallows into the mixture. Cover and place in the refrigerator; let chill overnight.
Top with whipped topping before serving.

Macaroni Salad

Serves 6–8

**BONNIE GASPARD
MAURICE, LOUISIANA**

1 (16-ounce) package elbow macaroni
2 cucumbers, diced small
1 large tomato, diced small
1 small green bell pepper, diced small
1 heaping tablespoon sour cream
3 heaping tablespoons mayonnaise
Salt and pepper, to taste

Cook macaroni according to package directions. Rinse and let drain. Mix the vegetables with macaroni. Stir in the sour cream and mix to combine. Stir in the mayonnaise and thoroughly combine. Season with salt and pepper. Let set for 1 hour in refrigerator before serving.

Cherry Coke Salad

Serves 10–12

JAMIE JO AXTELL
AXTELL CATTLE COMPANY
ANTON, COLORADO

1 (20-ounce) can crushed pineapple
½ cup water
2 small packages cherry or black cherry Jell-O
1 (21-ounce) can cherry pie filling
¾ cup Coke

Drain pineapple and reserve the juice. Mix reserved juice and water and bring to a boil. Add Jell-O and dissolve. Add cherry pie filling and Coke. Chill until soft set and then add pineapple. Chill until set.

Photo courtesy of Amber Johns.

Orange Jell-O Salad

Serves 8–10

LOU BASANEZ
MOUNTAIN CITY, NEVADA

1 (15.50-ounce) can crushed pineapple
1 large package orange Jell-O or any other gelatin
1 cup shredded coconut
2 cups buttermilk
1 cup pecan pieces
1 (12-ounce) container whipped topping

Pour pineapple and its juice into saucepan and bring to a boil. Remove from heat and stir in Jell-O until dissolved. Cool. Mix in coconut and buttermilk. Add pecans. Fold in whipped topping. Pour into a Bundt pan or ring mold that has been sprayed lightly with nonstick cooking spray. Refrigerate until set.

Orange-Tapioca Jell-O Salad

Serves 8–10

CARMA JOHNSON
AURORA, UTAH

      1 small box orange Jell-O
      1 small box cooked cook and serve vanilla pudding
      1 small box Americana tapioca pudding
      3 cups water
      9 ounces whipped topping
      4 (11-ounce) cans Mandarin oranges, drained

Combine Jell-O, puddings, and water in a saucepan and bring to a boil, stirring constantly. Continue to stir for 3 minutes or until tapioca balls start to turn transparent. Let cool, add whipped topping and stir together. Add Mandarin oranges. Refrigerate until firm.

You can substitute other flavors of Jell-O and fruit for a variation.

Side Dishes

Corn Casserole

Serves 6–8

**JESSIE MILLER
BRUNEAU, IDAHO**

1 (15.25-ounce) can whole-kernel corn, drained
1 (14.75-ounce) can cream-style corn
1 (8-ounce) package corn muffin mix (Jiffy)
1 cup sour cream
$1/2$ cup butter, melted
1 to 1 $1/2$ cups grated cheddar cheese

Preheat oven to 350 degrees and grease a 9 x 13-inch casserole dish.

In a large bowl, stir together the corn, muffin mix, sour cream, and butter. Pour into prepared casserole dish. Bake for 45 minutes, or until golden brown.

Remove from oven and top with cheese. Return to oven for 5–10 minutes, or until cheese is melted. Let stand for at least 5 minutes and then serve warm.

Onion Casserole

Serves 6–8

BONNIE GASPARD
MAURICE, LOUISIANA

3 onions, sliced, divided
1 regular-size bag Lays potato chips, divided
16 ounces grated cheddar cheese, divided
2 (10-ounce) cans condensed cream of mushroom soup
1 cup milk

Preheat oven to 350 degrees and butter a 9 x 13-inch casserole dish.
Using 1/4 of each of the first 3 ingredients, layer in the prepared dish. Repeat the layering 3 more times. Mix together the soup and milk and pour over the layers. Bake for 1 hour.

Italian Pasta Casserole

Serves 8–10

CAROL JOHNSON
JOHNSON LAND AND LIVESTOCK
RUSH VALLEY, UTAH

- 2 (16-ounce) packages penne pasta
- 2 (26-ounce) jars marinara sauce
- 3 (8-ounce) blocks mozzarella cheese, grated
- 1 quart whipping cream

Preheat oven to 350 degrees.

Cook pasta according to package directions. Drain and rinse in cold water, drain again.

In a 9 x 13-inch casserole dish, layer ingredients as follows: a thin layer of sauce on bottom, pasta, mozzarella, and then repeat. You should have about 3 layers each. Make sure to end with pasta on top. Pour the whipping cream all over the top. Pour slowly. Let it soak in.

Cover and bake for 1 hour or until hot in the middle. You can put more cheese on the top the last 20 minutes.

Alice Goicoechea's Garlic Spaghetti

Serves 6–8

MOLLY WOLF
WOLF AND SONS RANCHES
NORTH FORK, NEVADA

1 (16-ounce) package spaghetti
8 to 10 cloves garlic, finely chopped
Cooking oil
Salt and pepper, to taste
Parmesan cheese, to taste
Parsley

Cook spaghetti according to package directions. Just before you drain the spaghetti, fry the garlic to a golden brown in a generous amount of cooking oil. When the spaghetti is drained, place it in a serving dish. Pour cooked garlic and oil in spaghetti. Add salt and pepper and toss until well blended. Cover generously Parmesan cheese and sprinkle with parsley for a garnish.

Bull-Sale Beans

Makes a 12 inch Dutch Oven

MARK AND BECKY IPSEN
IPSEN CATTLE COMPANY
DINGLE, IDAHO
WWW.IPSENCATTLE.COM

Mark and I bring this dish to the presale social at the Utah Cattleman Classic Bull sale in Salt Lake City every December. The beans are a sure-fire hit and many people tell us how they look forward to them each year.

- 1 pound ground beef
- 1 kielbasa sausage, sliced
- 2 quarts cooked navy or pinto beans (you can used canned)
- 1 medium onion, diced
- 1 small to medium green bell pepper, diced
- 1/2 cup brown sugar
- 1 tablespoon prepared mustard
- 1 tablespoon Worcestershire sauce
- 1 (18–ounce) bottle barbecue sauce, of choice
- 1 cup water

Brown ground beef then add the rest of the ingredients. Simmer in a Dutch oven for 1–2 hours or until desired consistency.

IPSEN CATTLE COMPANY
DINGLE IDAHO
WWW.IPSENCATTLE.COM

7X

Ipsen Cattle Company has a long history in the Bear Lake Valley. Mark's great- grandfather, John Peter Ipsen, homesteaded land well over a century ago. This land is still part of our ranch operation. Mark took over operations when he was 23 years old and turned the previously commercial Hereford herd into a registered seed stock operation. We have sold Hereford and Angus bulls out of the Bear Lake Valley for 38 years now and hope to continue long into the future.

Photo courtesy of Amber Johns.

Cowboy Potatoes

Serves 6–8

DEBRA COCKRELL
COCKRELL RANCH & LODGING
CEDARVILLE, CALIFORNIA

    2 cups flour
    1 cup Parmesan cheese
    1/4 cup parsley flakes
    1 tablespoon granulated garlic
    1 teaspoon paprika
    Salt and pepper, to taste
    6 tablespoons melted butter
    8 red potatoes cut into 1-inch cubes or into rounds

Preheat oven to 400 degrees.

Place dry ingredients into a ziplock bag. Add melted butter to a baking sheet with sides. Rinse potatoes with cold water.

Add a handful of potatoes to the dry mixture and shake to coat well. Place on the baking sheet. Repeat until done. Bake for 30 minutes then turn potatoes. Bake for another 30 minutes or until golden in color and potatoes are tender.

Julie's Potatoes

Serves 8–10

BARBARA WOLF
WOLF AND SONS RANCHES
NORTH FORK, NEVADA

1 (1-pound) bag frozen southern-style hash brown potatoes, thawed
1 stick butter
2 cups condensed cream of chicken soup
1 pint sour cream
1/2 teaspoon salt
1 medium onion, chopped or 3/4 cup dried onion
2 cups grated longhorn or Colby cheese
2 cups crushed cornflakes
4 tablespoons butter, melted

Preheat oven to 350 degrees.

Place potatoes in a large bowl. Melt the stick of butter and pour into potatoes. Add soup, sour cream, salt, onion, and cheese. Mix well.

Place into a 9 x 13-inch baking dish. Cover with aluminum foil and bake for 45 minutes. When casserole is bubbly, uncover, spread on cornflakes and drizzle with the 4 tablespoons melted butter. Bake, uncovered, for 15 more minutes.

Roasted Baby Potatoes with Herbs

Serves 4–6

ED AND DEANA ALDER
HALE HOMESTEAD
TROUT CREEK, UTAH

1 pound small red-skinned potatoes, scrubbed
1 tablespoon herbes de Provence, plus extra for garnish
3 cloves garlic, minced
1/4 cup olive oil, plus extra for drizzling
Salt and freshly ground black pepper, to taste

Preheat oven to 400 degrees.

Place the potatoes in a large bowl. In a small bowl, whisk the herbs, garlic, and oil together until blended then pour over the potatoes. Sprinkle generously with salt and pepper and toss to coat. Transfer the potatoes to a large heavy baking dish, spacing them evenly apart.

Roast the potatoes until they are tender and golden, turning them occasionally with tongs, about 1 hour. Transfer the roasted potatoes to a decorative platter and drizzle with olive oil and herbes de Provence, if desired. Serve hot or warm.

Sweet Onion Potatoes Au Gratin

Serves 8–10

JESSIE MILLER
BRUNEAU, IDAHO

2 tablespoons butter
1 large or 2 medium Vidalia onions, thinly sliced
Salt and pepper, to taste
1/2 teaspoon ground or dried thyme
1 bay leaf
2 pounds baby Yukon gold potatoes
1/2 to 2/3 cup heavy cream
1/2 cup grated Parmigiano-Reggiano cheese
1/2 pound grated Guyere or other Swiss cheese

Heat butter in skillet over medium heat. Add onions, salt and pepper, thyme, and bay leaf. Cook until soft and lightly caramelized, about 20 minutes. Remove bay leaf.
While onions are cooking, boil potatoes in salted water for 12–15 minutes; drain. Mash potatoes with cream, season with salt and pepper, and mix in Parmigiano-Reggiano cheese.
Preheat broiler. Place potato mixture in a shallow casserole dish and top with onions and Guyere cheese. Brown under broiler for about 2 minutes.

Photo courtesy of Amber Johns.

Sweet Potato Souffle

Serves 8–10

**ED AND DEANA ALDER
HALE HOMESTEAD
TROUT CREEK, UTAH**

3 cups mashed sweet potatoes
2 eggs, beaten
1/2 teaspoon salt
1 cup sugar
1 teaspoon vanilla
1/2 cup milk
1 cup butter, melted, divided
1 cup packed dark brown sugar
1/3 cup flour
1 cup chopped pecans
1 cup shredded coconut

Preheat oven to 325 degrees.

In a large bowl, combine sweet potatoes, eggs, salt, sugar, vanilla, milk, and 2/3 cup butter. Blend until smooth and pour into 9 x 13-inch baking dish.

Prepare the topping by mixing together the brown sugar, flour, pecans, coconut, and remaining butter. Sprinkle mixture over potatoes. Bake for 30 minutes.

Yorkshire Pudding

Serves 10–12

BETH ANDERSON
WILLOW SPRINGS RANCH
CALLAO, UTAH

This recipe has been in the family for three generations. My grandpa, Cyrene Bagley, brought it back from England where he learned to love it as a missionary. We usually double the recipe and serve it with Sirloin tip roast and lots of gravy.

7/8 cup flour
1/2 teaspoon salt
1/2 cup milk
2 eggs, beaten
1/2 cup water
Hot beef drippings or butter

Sift flour and salt into a bowl. Make a well in the center, pour in milk and stir. Add eggs and water. Beat the batter well until large bubbles rise to the surface. Allow this to stand for 1 hour (optional) then beat it again.
Preheat oven to 400 degrees.
Have ready a hot 10 x 10-inch oven-proof dish or hot muffin tins containing about 1/4-inch hot beef drippings or melted butter. Pour in the batter. It should be about 5/8 inch high. Bake for about 20 minutes. Reduce the heat to 350 degrees and bake 10–15 minutes longer. Some people prefer to bake at 350 degrees for a half hour.

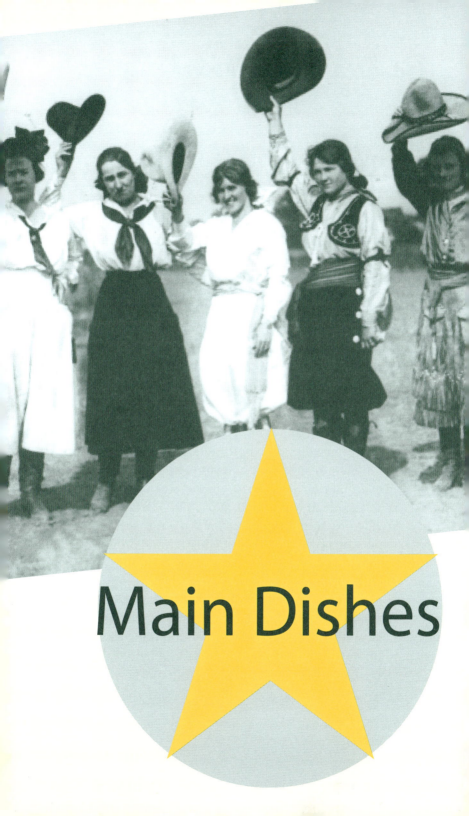

Main Dishes

Barbecue Beef Brisket

Serves 6–8

**DONA TULLIS
LONDON, OHIO**

Doris Bell is responsible for this wonderful recipe. It was the first place recipe in the 1977 Ohio Beef Cook-Off.

1 (5- to 6-pound) brisket
1 1/2 ounces liquid smoke
Celery salt, to taste
Onion salt, to taste
Garlic salt, to taste
2 tablespoons Worcestershire sauce
8 ounces barbecue sauce, of choice

Trim excess fat from the brisket. Place the meat in a roasting pan and pour the liquid smoke over the brisket. Generously sprinkle both sides of meat with celery, onion, and garlic salts. Cover tightly and refrigerate overnight.
When ready to roast, preheat oven to 325 degrees.
Pour Worcestershire sauce over brisket. Place aluminum foil over the top of the brisket and secure it around the outer edges of the roasting pan. Roast for 3 hours.
Remove from oven and pour off the excess liquid or transfer brisket to a smaller roasting pan. Pour barbecue sauce over the brisket. Cover top with foil, securing the edges around the pan, and cook for 1 additional hour. Allow the brisket to stand 1 hour after roasting before slicing. May be reheated in foil before serving.

Barbecue Beef Roast

Serves 4–6

**DONA TULLIS
LONDON, OHIO**

This is a recipe from Chris Acker from Wooster, Ohio.

1 (3- to 4-pound) beef roast
1 1/2 teaspoons salt
1/2 cup ketchup
1/4 cup vinegar
1/2 cup chopped onion
1 tablespoon Worcestershire sauce
1/4 teaspoon pepper

Preheat oven to 325 degrees.
Rub meat with salt. Place in an ungreased baking dish. Stir together remaining ingredients; pour over meat. Cover and bake oven for 3–4 hours until tender.

Barbecue Brisket

Serves 8

SHERRY SPENCER
SPENCER LAND & LIVESTOCK
YOST, UTAH

1 (2- to 2 1/2-pound) brisket, trimmed

Rub

- 1 teaspoon salt
- 1 teaspoon chili powder
- 1/2 teaspoon garlic powder
- 1/4 teaspoon onion powder
- 1/4 teaspoon celery salt
- 1/4 teaspoon pepper

Sauce

- 1/2 cup ketchup
- 1/2 cup chili sauce (Mae Ploy sweet chili sauce)
- 2 tablespoons cider vinegar
- 2 tablespoons Worcestershire sauce
- 1/2 teaspoon mustard powder
- 1/4 cup brown sugar

Combine rub ingredients and rub on brisket. Combine sauce ingredients. Place brisket in slow cooker or roaster. Pour 1/2 of the sauce over brisket, reserving 1/2 for serving. Cook on low for 10 hours in a slow cooker or 8–9 hours in a 200 degree oven in a roaster with a lid. Simmer remaining sauce 10 minutes and serve with brisket.

Easy Quantity Barbecue

Serves 20

**DONA TULLIS
LONDON, OHIO**

Dona was the 1983 and 1995 President of the Ohio CattleWomen (CowBelles). She is our current treasurer.

- 5 pounds ground beef
- 1 (27-ounce) can Manwich
- 1 (10.75-ounce) can condensed tomato soup
- 1 (10-ounce) jar pickle relish, do not drain
- 1 package onion soup mix (Lipton's)

Preheat oven to 350 degrees.

Brown beef in a large roaster in the oven, stirring often. This saves all the mess of browning on the top of the stove.

Drain off the fat; add rest of ingredients. Mix well and return to oven so flavors blend. Bake at least $1/2$ hour more. This recipe is easily doubled for a large crowd.

Barbecue Beef on a Roll

Serves 8

SHERRY SPENCER
SPENCER LAND & LIVESTOCK
YOST, UTAH

This was a winning recipe at the Utah Beef Cook-Off and received an honorable mention at National Beef Cook-Off.

- 3 pounds boneless beef chuck roast
- 2 tablespoons cooking oil
- 1 teaspoon seasoned salt
- 1/2 teaspoon pepper
- 3/4 cup apple juice
- 1 tablespoon flour
- 1 cup ketchup
- 2 tablespoons vinegar
- 4 tablespoons brown sugar
- 1 teaspoon Worcestershire sauce
- 1 teaspoon dry mustard
- 1 teaspoon celery salt
- 1 teaspoon paprika
- 1/2 cup chopped onion
- 8 sourdough rolls

Preheat oven to 325 degrees.

Brown both sides of roast in oil in a heavy roaster on stove top. Sprinkle both sides of meat with salt and pepper. Cover pan, place in oven, and cook for approximately 3 hours until meat shreds apart.

While roast is cooking, make the sauce. Place apple juice in a saucepan. Stir in flour and mix until well blended. Add the rest of the ingredients. Stir well and bring to boil then simmer 20 minutes. When roast is done, shred into small pieces. Add meat to sauce. Mix together well and simmer for 20 minutes. Serve on split rolls.

Barbecue Meatballs

Serves 8–10

JAMIE JO AXTELL
AXTELL CATTLE COMPANY
ANTON, COLORADO

Meatballs

1 1/2 pounds ground beef
2/3 cup evaporated milk
1 cup quick oatmeal
3/4 cup chopped onion
1/4 teaspoon pepper
1 egg, beaten
1 teaspoon salt
1 teaspoon chili powder

Sauce

1 cup ketchup
3/4 cup brown sugar
1/4 teaspoon garlic salt
1 tablespoon chopped onion
2 teaspoons liquid smoke

Preheat oven to 350 degrees.
Combine meatball ingredients by hand and shape into small meatballs (about the size of an ice cream scoop).
In separate bowl, mix sauce ingredients. Place meatballs in a 9 x 13-inch pan and pour sauce over them. Bake approximately 1 hour.

Photo courtesy of Amber Johns.

Cheesy Barbecue Sloppy Joes

Makes 16 servings

MARCUS BROUSSARD, TB CATTLE COMPANY, ESTHER, LOUISIANA

VICTORIA FREDERICK, BAR BAR F FARMS, ABBEVILLE, LOUISIANA

BRET LEE, LEE FAMILY FARM, ESTHER, LOUISIANA (2013 AND 2014 LOUISIANA BEEF AMBASSADOR)

This recipe started with a simple Sloppy Joe recipe, but was altered to add Cajun flavor with the use of locally produced barbecue sauce with a little "kick" and brown sugar to add sweetness. Marcus, Bret, and Victoria prepared this recipe for the Louisiana Cattlemen's Association Junior Beef Cook-Off and won the competition!

2 1/2 pounds lean ground beef
2 teaspoons salt
1 teaspoon red pepper
1/2 teaspoon black pepper
2 (14.5-ounce) cans diced tomatoes
2 cups ketchup
1 cup Jack Miller BBQ Sauce
1 cup Cattlemen's BBQ Sauce
1/2 cup brown sugar
2 packages frozen garlic Texas toast
1 cup grated mild cheddar cheese

Brown ground beef in a large skillet over medium heat. Add salt and peppers and stir often for 10 minutes or until beef crumbles and is no longer pink. Stir in tomatoes, ketchup, BBQ sauces, and brown sugar. Cook 15–20 minutes.

Meanwhile, prepare Texas toast according to package directions. Serve beef mixture over toast; sprinkle with cheese.

TB CATTLE COMPANY
ESTHER, LOUISIANA

Marcus is the son of Timothy and Gwen Broussard and is a fifth-generation cattleman. His family has been raising cattle in southern Vermilion Parish for over 100 years.

BAR BAR F FARMS
ABBEVILLE, LOUISIANA

Victoria is the daughter of Craig and Carleen Frederick and represents the fourth generation in her family to raise cattle in Abbeville, Louisiana. It began with a dairy and rice farm in the early 1960s and changed over to a commercial cow/calf herd and registered Brahman herd in the late 1970s.

LEE FAMILY FARM
ESTHER, LOUISIANA

Bret is the son of Al and Leisa Lee and he is a seventh-generation cattleman. His family grew rice and began raising cattle in Belle Isle (located in the marshes of southern Vermilion Parish) in the 1840s.

Creamy Crock-Pot Steak

Serves 8–10

MAGGIE MALSON
MALSON ANGUS & HEREFORDS
PARMA, IDAHO

My mom clipped this recipe from the *High Plains Journal* back in the 80s when us kids were growing up. It's still the meal I request when I take my family to visit my parents. It's the perfect meal for a fall or winter night. My kids love it, too! Plus, it's a great way to use a less expensive cut of meat.

- 2–3 pounds round steak
- 1/4 teaspoon salt
- 1 teaspoon pepper
- 1 teaspoon garlic powder
- 1 onion, chopped
- 1 green bell pepper, chopped
- 2 teaspoons Worcestershire sauce
- 2 (10.75-ounce) cans condensed cream soup (I use mushroom, but any kind works)
- Cooked rice

Cut steak into serving pieces and season with salt, pepper, and garlic powder. Place in Crock-Pot. Combine onion, bell pepper, Worcestershire sauce, and soup. Pour over meat and stir to completely coat. Cover and cook on high for 5–6 hours or 8–10 hours on low. Serve over rice.

Photo courtesy of Maggie Malson.

MALSON ANGUS & HEREFORDS
PARMA, IDAHO

Our ranch is a second-generation seed stock operation consisting of registered Angus and Hereford cattle. We sell range-ready bulls to commercial producers in the West. In addition, we have a productive cowherd and offer bred heifers, pairs, embryos, and show heifers to other purebred breeders during our fall production sale.

Rex's Recipe–Beef and Rice

Serves 2–4

JOAN SULLINGER
SULLINGER FARMS
RIDGEWAY, OHIO

My husband, Rex, developed this recipe while I was teaching school. Sometimes he had to fix the evening meal. It was easy and tasty.

1 (24-ounce) can canned beef
1 1/2 cups Minute Rice
Salt and pepper, to taste

Simmer beef in a medium saucepan. Add rice and stir. Add salt and pepper. Cover and let stand until rice is tender, about 5 minutes.

Beef Stroganoff

Serves 4–6

**ED AND DEANA ALDER
HALE HOMESTEAD
TROUT CREEK, UTAH**

2 pounds beef chuck roast
$1/2$ teaspoon salt
$1/2$ teaspoon ground black pepper
4 ounces butter
4 green onions, sliced (white parts only)
4 tablespoons all-purpose flour
1 (10.5-ounce) can condensed beef broth
1 teaspoon prepared mustard
1 (6-ounce) can sliced mushrooms, drained
$1/3$ cup sour cream
$1/3$ cup white wine
Salt, to taste
Freshly ground black pepper, to taste

Remove any fat and gristle from the roast and cut into strips $1/2$ inch thick by 2 inches long. Season strips with $1/2$ teaspoon of each salt and pepper.

In a large skillet over medium heat, melt the butter and brown the beef strips quickly then push the strips off to one side. Add the onions and cook slowly for 3–5 minutes then push to the side with the beef strips.

Stir the flour into the juices on the empty side of the pan. Pour in beef broth and bring to a boil, stirring constantly. Lower the heat and stir in mustard. Cover and simmer for 1 hour or until the meat is tender.

Five minutes before serving, stir in the mushrooms, sour cream, and wine. Heat briefly then season with salt and pepper.

Just a typical day around the Hale Homestead

Photos courtesy of the Alder family.

Crock-Pot Beef Eye of Round

Serves 4–6

BONNIE GASPARD
MAURICE, LOUISIANA

1 eye of round roast
10 cloves garlic, minced
Brown gravy packet, mixed
   (you can double or triple depending
   on how much gravy you want)

Place meat, garlic, and gravy in Crock-Pot and cook on low for 6–8 hours, or until tender. This is good served with rice and vegetables.

Variation: Add potatoes—place peeled and cubed potatoes in Crock-Pot for last hour of cooking time.

Crock-Pot Smothered Steak

Serves 4–6

RACHEL BUZZETTI
LAMOILLE, NEVADA

1/3 cup flour
1 teaspoon salt
1/4 teaspoon pepper
1 round steak
Canola oil
1 onion, diced
1 pound tomatoes or 1 (15-ounce)
  can tomato sauce or 1 (10.75-ounce)
  can condensed tomato soup
1 (4-ounce) can mushroom steak sauce
  (I use Dawn Fresh by Giorgio)
2 tablespoons molasses
3 tablespoons soy sauce

Mix flour, salt, and pepper together. Dust steak with flour mixture and brown in oil.
Place meat into Crock-Pot and add the remaining ingredients. Cook 6 hours on low.

Dutch Oven Beef Brisket

Serves 10

DARRELL JOHNSON
JOHNSON LAND AND LIVESTOCK
RUSH VALLEY, UTAH

>1 whole fresh beef brisket, not frozen, trimmed of all fat between layers
>Salt and pepper, to taste
>2 (12-ounce) cans Coke (not diet)
>2 packages onion soup mix
>2 cups ketchup

Season brisket with salt and pepper and place in a 12-inch Dutch oven. Mix Coke, soup mix, and ketchup together and pour over brisket. Cook for at least 4 hours on a slow fire or 4–5 hours in a 325 degree oven. Do not cook fast. Cut across the grain when cutting to serve.

Grandma Hammond's Casserole

Serves 6–8

RACHEL BUZZETTI
LAMOILLE, NEVADA

2 pounds ground beef
2 cloves garlic, minced
16 ounces tomato sauce
Salt and pepper, to taste
16 ounces wide egg noodles
2 bunches green onions, chopped
16 ounces cream cheese
2 cups sour cream
1 cup grated cheddar cheese

Preheat oven to 350 degrees.
In a frying pan, brown hamburger and garlic. Add tomato sauce, salt, and pepper. Set aside. Cook noodles according to package directions; drain and set aside.
In a large bowl, combine onions, cream cheese, and sour cream. Layer noodles, onion mixture, and meat in a 9 x 13-inch pan; repeat. Top with cheddar cheese and bake for 20–30 minutes.

Herb-Crusted Beef Roast

Serves 6–8

DR. SUZANNE MENGES
MENGES RANCH
GRAHAM AND GREENLEE COUNTIES, ARIZONA

This recipe was given to me by my mother-in-law, Billie Cloudt, when I was newly married.

- 1 (2- to 3-pound) beef rump roast
- Salt and pepper, to taste
- 1/4 cup chopped fresh parsley
- 1/4 cup chopped fresh oregano leaves
- 1/2 teaspoon dried rosemary leaves
- 1 teaspoon minced garlic
- 1 tablespoon vegetable oil
- 6 slices thick-cut bacon

Rub roast with salt and pepper. Combine next 5 ingredients and press into roast on top and sides.

Place roast in slow cooker. Place bacon on top of beef, tucking under, if needed. Cover and cook on low for 6–8 hours.

MENGES RANCH

Our ranch is located in southeastern Arizona in Greenlee and Graham counties. My sons (Ben is the one in the picture) are fifth-generation ranchers and our place is located on the historic Black Hills Back Country Byway. My husband and I have both served as state association presidents and region directors for NCBA (National Cattlemen's Beef Association) and ANCW (American National CattleWomen). Ben will take the reins of the Greenlee County Cattle Growers President next year—the first time a family has had three generations serve in that office.

Photos courtesy of Menges family.

Herbed Roasted Beef in Salt Crust

Serves 8–12

JESSIE MILLER
BRUNEAU, IDAHO

1/2 cup olive oil
1/4 cup grated onion
1 teaspoon garlic salt
1 teaspoon dried basil
1/2 teaspoon dried marjoram
1/2 teaspoon dried thyme
1/4 teaspoon pepper
1 (4- to 6-pound) boneless beef roast
1 (3-pound) box Morton's Coarse Kosher Salt
1 1/4 cups water

Combine oil, onion, and spices in a heavy ziplock bag. Mix well. Add roast and coat well with marinade. Marinate in refrigerator 2 hours or overnight.

Preheat oven to 425 degrees and line a roasting pan with aluminum foil.

Combine kosher salt and water to form a thick paste. Pat 1 cup paste into a $1/2$-inch-thick layer in pan. Pat roast dry with paper towels and insert meat thermometer. Place roast on salt layer and pack remaining salt paste around meat to seal well. Place roast in oven and roast 16–18 minutes per pound for rare (140 degrees), 20–22 minutes per pound for medium (160 degrees), or 25–30 minutes per pound for well done (170 degrees). Remove roast when thermometer registers 5 degrees below desired doneness.

Let roast stand for 5–10 minutes in salt crust before carving. Remove the roast from the salt; you may need to use a hammer. After removing crust, whisk away remaining crystals with a stiff pastry or vegetable brush. Slice and serve.

Use prime rib, eye of round, tenderloin, any heel roast of at least 4 pounds. If using a roast larger than 6 pounds, cooking time will not take as long as above guidelines. Bigger roasts are not necessarily larger around, just longer. A meat thermometer is absolutely essential to judge perfect cooking times.

Photo courtesy of Amber Johns.

Johnny Mazetti

Serves 8–10

CAROL JOHNSON
JOHNSON LAND AND LIVESTOCK
RUSH VALLEY, UTAH

4 slices bacon, chopped
3 onions, chopped
4 stalks celery, chopped
3 green bell peppers, chopped
6 cloves garlic, minced
2 (10-ounce) cans small mushrooms
2 pounds ground beef
Salt and pepper, to taste
16 ounces rotini noodles
1 (10.75-ounce) can condensed tomato soup
2 (15-ounce) cans tomato sauce
1 (10-ounce) can enchilada sauce
1 1/2 pounds grated cheddar cheese
2 (2.2-ounce) cans sliced black olives
2 dashes hot pepper sauce
2 teaspoons cumin

Preheat oven to 350 degrees.
Cook bacon in a large frying pan and then add onions, celery, bell peppers, garlic, and mushrooms; cook until vegetables are softened. Brown beef in another pan and drain. Cook noodles according to package directions and drain.
Mix everything together and then place in 2 (9 x 13-inch) casserole dishes. Cover and bake for 40–45 minutes.

Meatloaf or Meatballs and Gravy

Serves 6–8

DEBRA COCKRELL
COCKRELL RANCH & LODGING
CEDARVILLE, CALIFORNIA

2 pounds ground beef
1 pound ground pork sausage
2 eggs
¾ cup milk
½ cup ketchup
1 onion, chopped
5 slices white bread
2 teaspoons Worcestershire sauce
1 teaspoon garlic powder
1 teaspoon salt
1 teaspoon pepper

Gravy for Meatballs

2 (10.75-ounce) cans condensed cream of mushroom soup
2 cups milk
1 packet brown gravy mix

Preheat oven to 350 degrees and prepare a 9 x 13-inch baking dish with nonstick cooking spray.

In a large bowl, mix together ground beef and sausage. Whisk eggs, milk, and ketchup together in a separate bowl and pour over meat. Add onion to meat mixture. Stack sliced bread and cut into 1-inch pieces; add to the meat then add Worcestershire sauce, garlic powder, salt, and pepper.

Thoroughly combine meat mixture and place into prepared baking dish. Bake for 1 hour; 15 minutes before it's done, check and drain off any excess grease.

Meatballs: Make meatballs out of mixture and place them on a large baking sheet or in baking dishes. Bake at the same temperature as the meatloaf but for half the time. Drain off grease. In large skillet, combine soup, milk, and gravy mix. Bring to boil. Stirring, add cooked meatballs and simmer together for 15 minutes. Serve over mashed potatoes or white rice.

Meatballs for a Crowd

Serves 8–12

ROBIN LUFKIN
LUFKIN CATTLE CO
LEMHI, IDAHO

I make these quite often for brandings or when we ship and have a crowd, or I make the batch and just cook part of them at a time. Great for taking to others frozen and they can cook them when they need to.

Meatballs

3 pounds ground beef
1 (12-ounce) can evaporated milk
1 cup oatmeal
1 cup crushed cracker crumbs
2 eggs
1/2 cup chopped onion
1/2 teaspoon garlic powder
2 teaspoons salt
1/2 teaspoon pepper
2 teaspoons chili powder

Sauce

2 cups ketchup
1 cup brown sugar
1/2 teaspoon garlic powder
1/4 cup chopped onion
10 shakes Tabasco sauce

Meatballs: Mix all ingredients together, form into 1-inch balls, and place on a wax paper-covered baking sheet to freeze.
Sauce: Mix all sauce ingredients together.
After frozen, you can freeze the meatballs in ziplock bags until later or bake with sauce on them at 350 degrees for 1 hour.

Mexican Casserole

Serves 6–8

ELSIE W. FAREK
NAVIDAD RANCH
SCHULENBURG, TEXAS

This is a favorite at Navidad Valley CattleWomen potluck meetings.

1 pound ground beef, browned and grease drained
Salt and pepper, to taste
2 flour tortillas, torn into pieces
1 (15-ounce) can Ranch-Style beans
½ pound grated longhorn cheese
1 medium onion, chopped
2 flour tortillas, torn into pieces
1 (10.75-ounce) can condensed cream of chicken soup
1 (10-ounce) can Rotel tomatoes with green chiles, diced (I use mild)

Preheat oven to 350 degrees and grease a 9 x 13-inch casserole dish.
Layer ingredients in prepared casserole dish in the order given and bake for about 30 minutes, or until hot and bubbly.

No-Fail Beef Roast

Serves 4–6

**BARBARA WINTCH
WAH WAH RANCH
MANTI, UTAH**

Here is my no-fail beef roast for chuck, shoulder, or rump roast. My meat is usually frozen, so for Sunday dinner I take one of the mentioned above cuts out of the freezer and put it directly into my roasting pan to cook.

1 (3 1/2- to 5-pound) chuck, shoulder, or rump roast
3 tablespoons beef bouillon granules
1/4 cup water

Preheat oven to 350 degrees.
Take meat out of the freezer and place directly in a roasting pan. Sprinkle with bouillon and add water. Cover tightly and bake for 3 hours. The rump roast will need 1 hour longer. Monitor the meat closely after 3 hours.
Delicious gravy can be made from the drippings.

Poor Boys Shredded Beef

Serves 6–8

**TONYA LOHR
PARADISE CORNER FARM
BUCYRUS, OHIO**

This recipe is a hit with our Crawford County Cattleman's Association beef stand. It has been a family recipe for a few generations.

1 (3- to 4-pound) rump roast, thawed or frozen
1 teaspoon salt
3 large onions, sliced
1 1/2 teaspoons onion salt
1 1/2 teaspoons oregano
1/2 teaspoon garlic salt
1/2 teaspoon basil
1/2 teaspoon seasoned salt

Preheat oven to 250 degrees.

Place roast in pan filled half full of water. Sprinkle salt and onions over roast. Cook, uncovered, for 5–6 hours if thawed, or overnight if frozen.

Separate meat, onions, and broth. Pour broth into a saucepan and add onion salt, oregano, garlic salt, basil, and seasoned salt; stir to combine and keep warm while working with meat. Shred roast and place in a Crock-Pot with the broth and the onions that were over roast. For best results, puree onions first. Keep warm in the Crock-Pot when serving.

PARADISE CORNER FARM

My husband, Andy, and I purchased Paradise Corner Farm from my family. The farm has been in the family for well over a century. The farm had never been named until we purchased it and we came up with the name to tie both of our families together. My husband's parent's farm's name is Paradise Knoll and we live on a corner of our own little paradise.

The photos of the farm home shows its age and how we have tried to preserve our farm family history and look. We have also been successful with obtaining banners at the Ohio State Fair for three generations, starting with my grandfather Gail Crall taking carlots of 5. Andy then took pens of 3, and my daughter Jessica, with single entries of beef performance and carcass quality cattle. Our son Jake is hoping to follow in their footprints. Currently our farm consists of a cow/calf operation, feedlot, and club calves. Our hope is that our family will continue to farm and always have some type of beef operation.

Photos courtesy of the Lohr family.

Roast Beef Roll-ups

Serves 6–8

**JAMIE JO AXTELL
AXTELL CATTLE COMPANY
ANTON, COLORADO**

>Vegetable cream cheese
>Flour tortillas
>Grated cheddar cheese
>Grated carrot
>Deli roast beef
>Lettuce

Spread a thin layer of cream cheese on the tortilla. Cover with cheese, carrot, roast beef, and a lettuce leaf. Roll tightly and wrap in foil. Refrigerate at least 4 hours before serving for best taste. They can be served plain or with dressing, I prefer dipping mine in Dorothy Lynch Salad Dressing.

Steak from the Grill

Serves 1

SA WALKUP
GLADHOUR FARM
WHEELING, MISSOURI

Use a steak from a grass-only Dexter who has achieved roughly 650 pounds live weight before slaughter. Have the steaks cut to your personal preference, but I recommend 1 1/2- to 2-inches thickness. The steak can be boneless or bone-in. If frozen, thaw the steak in the refrigerator then bring to room temperature before grilling.

I provided such Dexter steaks to a local grazing group's cook-off where a local chef prepared them the same way. This recipe describing his method came from the chef. The Dexter steaks were proclaimed tender, delicious, and the way grass-fed should be pretty much all around the table.

1 (1 1/2- to 2-inch-thick) grass-fed Dexter steak, of choice
Coarse sea salt, to taste
Freshly ground black pepper
Garlic powder, to taste, optional

Prepare the grill to a good cooking heat (in between the first flaming stage and cooling coals).
Salt and pepper both sides of the steak (I had understood that salting ahead draws too much of the moistness out of the meat, but this recipe has been great tasting, so now this is the cooking I prefer.)
Place steak on grill and sear for 3–4 minutes. When the bubbles of moisture appear, you can check to see if you have a nice sear on the first side. If so, flip the steak to the second side and sear for 3–4 minutes. When little oozing of blood appears on the top, you can remove the steak. If you like the steak medium rare to medium, remove it from the grill at this point and place in a pan that is already warmed to an approximately equal temperature, cover lightly with foil, and allow the steak to rest before being served.

GLADHOUR FARM
WHEELING, MISSOURI

Gladhour Farm is located in the gently rolling rich farmland of northern Missouri. It is a family farm, in the same family since the 1800s.

The farming plan is sustainable agriculture: row crops are certified organic; veal and beef are raised naturally on cow's milk and forage with no added hormones or subtherapeutic antibiotics and no GMOs; and heritage breeds (Irish Dexter cattle and Babydoll Southdown sheep) are raised for breeding stock and enjoyment. In addition, historical landmarks, roadways, equipment, buildings, and plants are valued to give visitors glimpses of times gone by and lifestyles which have something worthwhile to offer us today by way of balance and learning.

A stage coach line and later "Old Number 8—Pike's Peak Ocean to Ocean Highway," the nation's early transcontinental highway, ran through what is now Gladhour Farm. A major Chautauqua ground was nearby from the late 1800s through early 1900s.

Photo courtesy of SA Walkup.

Taco Calzones

Serves 4

SUE MOSSER
MOSSER RANCH
MEDORA, NORTH DAKOTA

1 (4-ounce) can diced green chiles
1/4 cup water
1/2 or 1 package taco seasoning, to taste
1 pound ground beef, browned
1 package (2 crusts) refrigerated pie crust
1 cup grated Colby, Jack or cheddar cheese

Preheat oven to 425 degrees.
Add chiles, water, and taco seasoning to browned beef. Mix well.
Cut pie crusts in half. Place 1/2 cup of the beef filling on each half of the pie crusts. Place 1/4 cup cheese on top of each. Dampen edge of crusts with water. Fold sides over filling and crimp edges with fork. Place on ungreased baking sheet and bake for 12 minutes.

MOSSER RANCH
MEDORA, NORTH DAKOTA

The Mosser Ranch was purchased in 1950 by Randy Mosser's grandfather, Ralph. Randy's dad leased the ranch from 1950–1966 and his brother, Doug, bought the ranch from Ralph in 1973. In 1995, Doug moved to his dad's ranch and leased his half to Randy and Sue Mosser.

Photo courtesy of Amber Johns.

Bonnie's Beef Pepper Steak

Serves 2–4

GENE AND BONNIE OSTLER
OSTLER'S SHOW STEERS
ROOSEVELT, UTAH

1 1/2 pounds steak, of choice (sirloin, flat iron, etc), diced
1 yellow onion, chopped
Garlic salt, to taste
Pepper, to taste
1 (4-ounce) can diced green chiles
1 (10-ounce) can Mexican diced tomatoes with green chiles
3 to 4 beef bouillon cubes
2 cloves garlic, minced
1 (6.5-ounce) can mushrooms
1 to 2 green bell peppers, sliced
Rice or noodles, cooked

Brown the steak with onion, garlic salt, and pepper. Add green chiles and tomatoes, and using the tomato can, add 2 to 3 cans of water, the bouillon cubes, garlic, and mushrooms. Simmer for 1 hour or until steak is tender. Add the bell peppers and simmer for 15 more minutes. Thicken a little with cornstarch. Serve over rice or noodles.

Amaretto Cake

Serves 10–12

CLAUDETTE BROUSSARD
VERMILION PARISH CATTLEWOMEN
COLUMBUS PLANTATION
ABBEVILLE, LOUISIANA

1 box butter cake mix
4 eggs
1 cup sour cream
1 cup amaretto
1/2 cup vegetable oil
1 cup chopped pecans

Preheat oven to 350 degrees and grease and flour a Bundt pan.

Combine cake mix, eggs, sour cream, amaretto, and oil. Beat with mixer on medium speed for 5 minutes. Add pecans; stir well.

Pour into prepared pan and bake for 55–60 minutes or until toothpick inserted in center comes out clean. Remove from oven and cool for 30 minutes. Remove cake from pan and cool completely on a wire rack. Frost with cream cheese frosting or dust with confection sugar.

Chocolate Zucchini Cake

Serves 8–10

JAMIE JO AXTELL
AXTELL CATTLE COMPANY
ANTON, COLORADO

This recipe was handed down from my great-aunt, Evelyn.

- 1/2 cup butter
- 1 3/4 cups sugar
- 1/2 cup vegetable oil
- 2 eggs
- 1 teaspoon vanilla
- 1/2 cup sour milk (milk with a dash of white vinegar)
- 2 1/2 cups flour
- 1/2 teaspoon baking powder
- 1/2 teaspoon ground cloves
- 4 tablespoons cocoa powder
- 1 teaspoon baking soda
- 1/2 teaspoon cinnamon
- 2 cups shredded zucchini
- Chocolate chips, of choice

Preheat oven to 325 degrees and grease a 9 x 13-inch pan. Cream butter, sugar, and oil. Add eggs, vanilla, and milk. Stir in dry ingredients and then zucchini. Pour into prepared pan and top with chocolate chips. Bake for 40–45 minutes.

Grandma Wolf's Whipped Cream Chocolate Cake

Servings: 8–10

MOLLY WOLF
WOLF AND SONS RANCHES
NORTH FORK, NEVADA

This recipe came to me from my mother-in-law. Her mother-in-law is the creator behind the recipe. It is one of the best chocolate cakes you will ever eat!

1 cup sour cream
2 eggs
1 cup sugar
1 teaspoon vanilla
1 1/2 cups flour
1/2 teaspoon salt
1 teaspoon baking soda
1/2 cup boiling water
2 squares chocolate, melted

Preheat oven 350 degrees.
Whip sour cream until firm, add eggs, and whip until well blended. Add sugar, beat again, and add vanilla, flour, and salt.
Dissolve baking soda in boiling water and add it with the melted chocolate to the whipped cream mixture.
Pour batter into an 8 x 8-inch pan and bake for 20 minutes or until toothpick comes out clean.

Photo courtesy of the Wolf family.

Great-Grandmother's Nut Cake

Serves 10–12

CAROL JOHNSON
JOHNSON LAND AND LIVESTOCK
RUSH VALLEY, UTAH

This recipe goes way back to Denmark. My family, the Monsens, brought it with them as pioneers.

Cake

- 1/2 cup butter
- 1 cup whipping cream
- 1 cup sugar
- 2 cups flour
- 2 teaspoons baking powder
- 1/4 teaspoon salt
- 1 cup milk
- 5 egg whites, stiffly beaten
- 1 cup roughly chopped walnuts

Frosting

- 1 cup sugar
- 1/2 cup whole milk
- 1 to 2 teaspoons vanilla, orange, or lemon flavoring, to taste

Cake: Preheat oven to 350 degrees and grease and flour a Bundt pan.

Beat butter and whipping cream together until thick. Add sugar.

Sift together flour, salt, and baking powder. Alternately add to butter mixture with milk. Fold egg whites into the batter and then fold in the nuts. Pour into prepared pan and bake for 40–45 minutes.

Frosting: Combine sugar and milk together and boil for 5 minutes at a full boil. Whip, add the flavoring of your choice, and frost the cake.

JOHNSON LAND AND LIVESTOCK
RUBY VALLEY, UTAH

Our ranch is located in western Utah approximately 60 miles southwest of Salt Lake City. It was established in 1856 by Luke Johnson. We now have the seventh generation of family living here. We run cattle mostly on private land where we have implemented many ranch improvement practices to be able to increase our carrying capacity. Our brand was used in the earliest years before Utah required a brand registry. Our cattle herd is primarily Angus-Hereford crosses which do very well in our semi-desert area. We are thankful and proud that we are able to continue a ranching heritage that has been carried out through so many generations.

Hot-Water Chocolate Cake

Serves 8–10

BILLIE SUE SLAGOWSKI
SLAGOWSKI RANCHES, INC.
PINE VALLEY, NEVADA

I remember my mom, Grace, always made this cake when my grandfather and his wife came to visit. It was Sissie's favorite.

> 1 cup sugar
> 1/2 cup shortening
> 2 eggs
> 1/3 cup cocoa powder
> 1 1/4 cups flour
> 1 teaspoon baking soda
> 1/2 cup sour milk
> 1/2 cup hot water

Preheat oven to 350 degrees and grease an 8 x 8-inch pan.
Cream sugar and shortening together. Add eggs.
Sift flour, baking soda, and cocoa powder together. Add to the sugar mixture, alternating with milk. Add water last, a third at a time. Pour batter into the prepared pan and bake for 35 minutes.

Poor Man's Cake

Serves 10–12

CAROL JOHNSON
JOHNSON LAND AND LIVESTOCK
RUSH VALLEY, UTAH

I received this recipe from my mother-in-law. It was popular during the depression and World War II because it didn't call for any eggs or butter. This is a heavy cake. You do not need frosting, but you can use a cream cheese frosting, if desired.

2 cups sugar (can use 1 cup sugar and 1 cup honey)
3 cups raisins
3 cups water
¾ cup shortening
4 cups flour
1 teaspoon salt
2 teaspoons baking powder
2 teaspoons baking soda
2 teaspoons cloves
2 teaspoons cinnamon
1 teaspoon nutmeg
1 to 2 cups nuts, of choice

Preheat oven to 350 degrees and grease a 9 x 13-inch pan.
Boil the sugar and raisins in the water for 3 minutes to soften. Add shortening to raisins and water. Let cool slightly.
Sift together flour, salt, baking powder, baking soda, cloves, cinnamon, and nutmeg. Mix flour mixture into raisin mixture. Fold in nuts, if using. The batter will be thin. Pour into prepared pan and bake for 35–40 minutes. Check at 34 minutes.

Toasted Almond Chocolate Bar Cake

Serves 12

BETTY GARNER
CRYSTAL ACRES FARM
DANVILLE, ARKANSAS

Cake

1/2 cup vegetable oil
1 1/4 cups water
3 eggs
1 box Swiss chocolate cake mix

Frosting

1 (8-ounce) block cream cheese
1 cup sugar
1 cup powdered sugar
1 (8-ounce) container whipped topping
6 to 8 ounces sliced toasted almonds
1 (8-ounce) chocolate bar, chopped or chocolate chips or chopped chocolate kisses

Cake: Preheat oven to 350 degrees and prepare 2 (9-inch) cake pans with nonstick cooking spray.
Combine oil, water, eggs, and cake mix and evenly divide between prepared pans. Bake for 30 minutes, or until done. Cool in pans for 10 minutes and then invert onto wire racks to completely cool.
Frosting: Beat cream cheese and sugar together then beat in powdered sugar until creamy. Stir in the whipped topping and then stir in about half of the almonds and all the chocolate.
Frost the cooled cake and press the remaining almonds on the top and sides of the cake. Refrigerate.

Raw Apple Cake

Serves 20

JACKIE SLAVICK
SLAVICK FARM AND RANCH
NEW SALEM, NORTH DAKOTA

I have used this recipe since 1955 when I was a junior in high school. I got it from the mother of a friend after having it for an after-school snack at her home.

2 cups sugar
2 eggs
1 cup margarine, softened
1 cup cold coffee
3 cups flour
2 teaspoons baking powder
1 teaspoon cinnamon
1/2 teaspoon salt
1 teaspoon baking soda
1/2 teaspoon cloves
1/2 teaspoon nutmeg
1 cup raisins
1 cup chopped apple, with skin
1 cup chopped walnuts

Preheat oven to 350 degrees and grease a 9 x 13-inch pan. Mix sugar, eggs, and margarine until blended. Add coffee and then gradually add flour and other ingredients. Pour into the prepared pan and bake for 45–50 minutes.

SLAVICK FARM AND RANCH
NEW SALEM, NORTH DAKOTA

Our ranch was declared a centennial farm and ranch in 1989 by the North Dakota Agriculture Department. Great-granddad Joseph Slavick came to America at the age of 14 from Czechoslovakia in 1886. He and a 19-year-old brother were the only ones from his family to come. We have never known what became of his parents. The brothers first came to Minnesota for a short time before they homesteaded in North Dakota. Since then the ranch has been owned and operated by five generations from father to son. Each generation has added more acres and cattle through the years. Since Joseph Slavick, there have been William Sr., Robert E., Robert J., and Robert D. I am the wife of Robert E. and we have been married for 54 years and still help our son. The ranch is now owned and operated by the three Roberts. The ranch produces beef cattle and small grains.

Rhubarb Cake

Serves 8–10

BILLIE SUE SLAGOWSKI
SLAGOWSKI RANCHES, INC.
PINE VALLEY, NEVADA

I received this recipe from my sister Aulene. My husband, who doesn't care for rhubarb, likes this cake.

1 1/2 cups sugar
1/2 cup shortening
1 egg, beaten
1 cup sour cream or buttermilk or sour milk
2 cups flour
1 teaspoon baking soda
1/4 teaspoon salt
1 teaspoon vanilla
2 cups diced rhubarb
1/4 cup sugar combined with 2 teaspoons cinnamon

Preheat oven 350 degrees and grease and flour a 9 x 13-inch pan.
Cream sugar and shortening together. Add egg and sour cream. Combine flour, baking soda, and salt together and mix in creamed mixture. Stir in vanilla and add rhubarb.
Pour into the prepared pan and sprinkle the sugar and cinnamon mixture over the top. Bake for 30–35 minutes.

Coconut Custard Pie

Serves 6–8

RACHEL BUZZETTI
LAMOILLE, NEVADA

This recipe came from my grandma, Tillie Zimmerman.

- 2 cups milk
- 1/2 cup Bisquick
- 1/4 cup butter
- 3/4 cup sugar
- 3 eggs
- 1 teaspoon vanilla
- 1 cup shredded coconut

Preheat oven to 350 degrees and grease a pie plate.
Place milk, Bisquick, butter, sugar, eggs, and vanilla in a blender and blend for 3 minutes. Add coconut to the blender and blend just until mixed. Let mixture stand in blender for 5 minutes. Then pour into prepared pie plate and bake for 30 minutes.

DISASTER PEAK RANCH

On June 25, 1950, my grandparents Evan and Tillie Zimmerman, with three small children in tow (Ross, Ted, and Dennis), traversed the Sierras, left California, the only area they had ever known, and moved to a spot just west of the middle of nowhere, beneath Disaster Peak. The Disaster Peak Ranch is still owned and operated by the Zimmerman family.

Photos courtesy of Rachel Buzzetti.

Quick Fruit Cobbler

Serves 6–8

BILLIE SUE SLAGOWSKI
SLAGOWSKI RANCHES, INC.
PINE VALLEY, NEVADA

This is a great recipe to whip up on those days that are very busy, or for unexpected company.

- 1/2 cup butter
- 1 cup flour
- 1 cup sugar
- 1 cup milk
- 1 teaspoon baking powder
- 1/4 teaspoon salt
- 1 (15-ounce) can of your choice of fruit, drained

Preheat oven to 400 degrees and melt butter in an 8 x 11-inch baking dish.

Mix flour, sugar, milk, baking powder, and salt in a bowl. Blend well and pour over melted butter. Add fruit. Bake for 25–30 minutes.

Peach Crumb Bars

Serves 8–10

ROBIN LUFKIN
LUFKIN CATTLE CO.
LEMHI, IDAHO

Dough

    3 cups flour
    1 cup sugar
    1 teaspoon baking powder
    1/2 teaspoon salt
    2 sticks butter, cut into small pieces
    2 tablespoons whipping cream

Peach Filling

    5 cups diced peaches
    1/2 cup flour
    1 cup sugar
    1/4 teaspoon salt
    1/2 teaspoon cinnamon
    1/4 teaspoon nutmeg

Preheat oven to 375 degrees.

Dough: Combine flour, sugar, baking powder, and salt in a bowl and then cut in butter until it resembles cornmeal. Add enough cream to make the dough come together like you are making pie crust. Pat most of the dough into a 9 x 13-inch pan, reserving a small amount for the top.

Peach Filling: Mix filling ingredients together and pour over dough. Crumble the remaining dough over the filling and bake for 45 minutes.

Cowboy Cookies

Makes 3–4 dozen

**JESSIE MILLER
BRUNEAU, IDAHO**

¾ cup pecans
1 cup unsalted butter, softened
¾ cup sugar
¾ cup packed light brown sugar
2 large eggs
1 teaspoon vanilla
2 cups flour
1 teaspoon baking soda
1 teaspoon salt
½ teaspoon baking powder
1 ½ cups old-fashioned oats
6 ounces semisweet chocolate chips
½ cup unsweetened shredded coconut

Preheat oven to 350 degrees. Spray baking sheets with nonstick cooking spray, line with parchment paper, and spray paper.
Toast pecans for 10–13 minutes on another baking sheet. Cool and coarsely chop.
Using an eclectic mixer on medium speed, cream butter and sugars together until pale and fluffy. Reduce speed and add eggs, 1 at a time, beating well after each addition. Beat in vanilla.
Combine flour, baking soda, salt, and baking powder in another bowl. Add flour mixture to butter mixture and beat until incorporated. Beat in chocolate, pecans, and coconut until combined. Drop dough onto prepared baking sheets using a 1 ½-inch ice cream scoop or tablespoon about 3 inches apart.
Bake for 16–18 minutes until edges begin to brown. Transfer to wire racks to cool, about 5 minutes.

Fig Cookies

Makes 4–5 dozen

BONNIE GASPARD
MAURICE, LOUISIANA

2 cups sugar
1 stick butter, softened
3 eggs
1 teaspoon baking soda
1 teaspoon cinnamon
3 cups flour
1 cup nuts, of choice
1 1/2 cups fig preserves

Preheat oven to 350 degrees.
Combine sugar, butter, and eggs together in a large bowl. In another bowl, mix baking soda, cinnamon, and flour; add to the butter mixture. Stir in nuts and preserves.
Drop by spoonfuls on a baking sheet and bake for 10–13 minutes.

Photo courtesy of Amber Johns.

Traditional Sugar Cookies

Makes 4 dozen

MOLLY WOLF
WOLF AND SONS RANCHES
NORTH FORK, NEVADA

> 3/4 cup shortening (or part butter)
> 1 cup sugar
> 2 eggs
> 1 teaspoon vanilla
> 2 1/2 cups flour
> 1 teaspoon baking powder
> 1 teaspoon salt

Easy Creamy Frosting

> 1 cup powdered sugar
> 1/2 teaspoon vanilla
> 1/4 teaspoon salt
> 1 to 2 tablespoons half-and-half

Thoroughly mix shortening, sugar, eggs, and vanilla. Blend in flour, baking powder, and salt. Cover and chill for at least 1 hour.

Preheat oven at 400 degrees.

Roll dough to a 1/4-inch thickness on a floured board and cut out cookies using your favorite shapes. Place on an ungreased baking sheet and bake for 6–8 minutes, or until lightly browned. Cool and frost with Easy Creamy Frosting.

Easy Creamy Frosting: Mix powdered sugar, vanilla, and salt. Stir in half-and-half until frosting is smooth and of spreading consistency.

Chocolate Dessert

Serves 8–10

GERI VAN NORMAN
VAN NORMAN RANCHES, INC.
VAN NORMAN QUARTER HORSES, INC.
TUSCARORA, NEVADA

Crust

1 cup flour
1 stick butter
1 cup chopped nuts, of choice

Cream Cheese Layer

1 (8-ounce) block cream cheese, softened
1 cup powdered sugar
$1/2$ (9-ounce) container whipped topping, reserve remaining topping

Topping

1 small box vanilla instant pudding
1 small box chocolate instant pudding
3 cups milk
Grated chocolate or chopped nuts

Crust: Preheat oven to 350 degrees.

Mix flour, butter, and nuts together. Press into a 9 x 13-inch ungreased pan and bake for 15 minutes. Let cool.

Cream Cheese Layer: Beat cream cheese and sugar together. Add whipped topping and spread over cooled crust.

Topping: Mix together the puddings. Add milk and beat for 2 minutes. Spread over cream cheese layer. Place in refrigerator until set. Then spread with reserved whipped topping and decorate with grated chocolate or chopped nuts.

VAN NORMAN RANCHES, INC. AND VAN NORMAN QUARTER HORSES, INC. TUSCARORA, NEVADA

Charlie and Della Van Norman bought a small homestead in the Independence Valley, near Tuscarora in 1945. Both of them had ranching heritages. Della was born and raised in the same valley on a neighboring ranch. Together they created a ranching enterprise that lasted their entire lifetime. Today, the families now own and operate Van Norman Ranches, Inc. and Van Norman Quarter Horses, Inc. as independent entities.

Cream Puffs

Makes 10–12 puffs

MOLLY WOLF
WOLF AND SONS RANCHES
NORTH FORK, NEVADA

1 cup water
1/2 cup butter
1 cup flour
4 eggs
Pudding, of choice
Powdered sugar

Preheat oven to 400 degrees.
Heat water and butter to a boil and then add flour all at once. Stir until it leaves the sides of the pan. Stir in eggs, 1 at a time. Drop spoonfuls onto a baking sheet and bake for 45–50 minutes. Crack open the oven door and leave puffs in the oven to cool slowly.
When completely cool, cut in half and fill one half with your favorite pudding. Put tops back on and dust with powder sugar.

Hedge Hog

Serves 4–6

**RACHEL BUZZETTI
BUZZETTI RANCHES
LAMOILLE, NEVADA**

Betsy McFarlane gave me this recipe. It is definitely one for those who love chocolate.

> 3 sticks butter
> 1 $^1/_2$ cups sugar
> 6 tablespoons cocoa powder
> 3 teaspoons vanilla
> 3 eggs, beaten
> 1 $^1/_2$ packages rich tea biscuits, ground

In a large saucepan, melt butter and then stir in sugar and cocoa. Add vanilla and eggs and bring to a boil. Mix in biscuits. Press into a 9 x 9-inch pan to set up. Slice into bars.

Waverly Pecan Treats

Serves 10

BONNIE GASPARD
MAURICE, LOUISIANA

1 sleeve of Waverly crackers (buttered crackers)
2 sticks butter
1 cup sugar
1 cup ground pecans

Preheat oven to 350 degrees and line the bottom and sides of a baking sheet with aluminum foil.
Place crackers on bottom of pan end to end. Heat butter, sugar, and pecans in a saucepan until melted and thoroughly combined. Pour over crackers.
Bake for 20 minutes, or until golden brown. Cool and snap apart.

Aunt Mickey's Honey Candy

MARLENE BAGLEY
BETH ANDERSON
WILLOW SPRINGS RANCH
CALLAO, UTAH

My Aunt Mickey (Marlene Bagley) would make this for us after my dad had given her some cream from the cow he milked twice daily. She would fill the empty cream bottle with the wrapped candy, which we loved to receive.

1/2 cup honey
1/2 cup heavy cream
2 cups sugar
Vanilla, to taste

Combine honey, cream, and sugar and cook to a hard ball stage. It will turn a light brown. Pour onto a buttered dish and stretch; let cool. I usually use 2 buttered bread loaf pans, or if I double the batch, I use a buttered 9 x 13-inch pan. When it is cool enough to handle, start to pull. Put vanilla in while you're stretching it. It will stretch to a nice white creamy color. Lay it out on wax paper in a long rope. While it is still warm, mark it with a table knife then turn over and tap on the back of the mark to break it. Wrap pieces in wax paper.

Peanut Brittle

Makes about 2 pounds

BILLIE SUE SLAGOWSKI
SLAGOWSKI RANCHES, INC.
PINE VALLEY, NEVADA

This recipe came to me in the chain letters that were popular a while ago. I make this candy every Christmas.

2 cups sugar
1 cup Karo syrup
1 cup water
1 cup raw peanuts
1 tablespoon butter
1 teaspoon vanilla
2 teaspoons baking soda

Boil sugar, syrup, and water until it reaches 240 degrees on a candy thermometer. Then add peanuts and boil until 300 degrees.
Add butter, vanilla, and baking soda. Spread in a large greased pan and stretch it. Cool and break into pieces.

Good Popcorn

Serves 4–6

**RACHEL BUZZETTI
LAMOILLE, NEVADA**

3 bags microwave popcorn, popped
3 cups mini marshmallows
1 cup butter
1 1/3 cups sugar
1/2 cup light corn syrup
1 teaspoon vanilla

Mix popcorn and marshmallows together in a large bowl. Melt butter, sugar, and syrup in medium saucepan and bring to a boil. Turn heat down and simmer for 3 minutes. Remove from heat and stir in vanilla. Pour over popcorn and marshmallows and stir well. The sauce will melt the marshmallows and make it gooey.

Caramel Popcorn

Serves 4–6

SHERRY SPENCER
SPENCER LAND & LIVESTOCK
YOST, UTAH

2 sticks butter
1 cup brown sugar
1/2 cup Karo syrup
1/2 teaspoon maple extract
1/8 teaspoon salt
7 to 8 cups popped popcorn
Peanuts, optional

Preheat oven to 250 degrees and prepare 2 baking sheets with nonstick cooking spray.

Bring butter, brown sugar, syrup, maple extract, and salt to a boil in a heavy saucepan. Lower heat and simmer for 5 minutes. Pour over popcorn and stir until well covered. Add peanuts, if using. Spread popcorn on prepared baking sheets and bake for 1 hour. Remove popcorn from baking sheets while warm.

Bagged Ice Cream

Serves 4–6

**GINGER JOHNSON
JOHNSON MOUNTAIN RANCH
AURORA, UTAH**

1 cup milk
1 cup whipping cream
1/2 cup sugar
1/2 teaspoon vanilla
Fruit or candy

Place all ingredients into a 1-quart ziplock bag and seal. Put the quart bag in a 1-gallon ziplock bag and surround with ice and rock salt. Seal well—I duct tape it shut. Duct tape layers of newspaper around the gallon bag and toss back and forth until frozen. This is a great outdoor activity and it is yummy!

Beignets

Serves 10–12

BONNIE GASPARD
MAURICE, LOUISIANA

2 cups flour
1/2 teaspoon salt
1/2 teaspoon baking soda
2 teaspoon baking power
1 egg
Milk
Syrup or powdered sugar

Combine dry ingredients and stir in egg. Add enough milk to get the consistency of pancake patter. Drop by spoonfuls into hot grease and fry until browned. Serve with syrup or powdered sugar.

This and That

To Make Butter

AMBER JOHNS
ELKO, NEVADA

This recipe was taken out of the *Reflections Cookbook, Bicentennial–Centennial 1976*, Custer County, Colorado. This cookbook contains many of my grandmother's and aunts' recipes. This is one that always makes me think of my grandmother.

Scald the churn thoroughly then cool well with spring water. Next pour in the thick cream. Churn fast at first, then, as the butter forms, more slowly; always with perfect regularity. In warm weather, pour a little cold water into the churn should the butter form slowly. In the winter, use warm water for the same purpose. When the butter has "come" rinse the blades of the churn down with cold water and take up the butter with a wooden ladle. When you have collected all the butter, drain off excess water, squeezing and pressing the butter with a ladle until all milk is removed. Add a little salt and mold or put in pats.

Steak Marinade

Makes 4 cups

CLAUDETTE BROUSSARD
VERMILION PARISH CATTLEWOMEN
COLUMBUS PLANTATION
ABBEVILLE, LOUISIANA

> 2 (10-ounce) bottles soy sauce
> 1/2 (16-ounce) bottle water
> 1/2 cup honey
> 1/2 cup chopped green onions
> 5 cloves garlic, chopped
> 1 tablespoons meat tenderizer

Mix all ingredients together. Place steaks in large deep dish. Pour marinade over steaks. Marinate for no longer than 2 hours, turning steaks over after first hour. Remove from marinade and season steaks, to taste. Grill steaks and enjoy.

COLUMBUS PLANTATION
ABBEVILLE, LOUISIANA

Our farm/ranch has been in my husband's family for three generations. His grandfather started it raising commercial cattle and planting rice. His father continued this process until he retired. My husband dropped the rice farming and raised a small herd of commercial and registered Brangus cattle until he retired. We now grow crawfish on the farm.

Chutney

BRENDA HART
HARRIS/HART RANCH
CLE ELUM, WASHINGTON

The Newton family had Chutney on the table for every meal—breakfast, lunch, and dinner.

6 pounds ripe tomatoes
3 pounds green apples
2 pounds onions
1 pint vinegar
2 pounds sugar
1/2 teaspoon cayenne
1/4 cups salt
2 teaspoons cinnamon

After peeling, grind all vegetables. Stir in other ingredients. Use large canner and cook over medium heat, stirring frequently. When the water boils, cook 2 more hours on low. Can in quart or pint jars. Boil jar lids, fill hot jars with Chutney, and tightly seal.

Photos courtesy of the Hart Family.

NEWTON RANCH
CLE ELUM, WASHINGTON

Ernest and Mary Newton moved to Cle Elum in 1902 and purchased the John McDonald ranch. This ranch remained in the Newton family for over seventy years. The land had to be cleared; stumps were grubbed out by hand. Whenever

equipment broke down, Ernest would walk to Cle Elum, five miles away, to get a replacement. By 1926 the family had cleared 160 acres for pasture and cultivation. They had ten children, and as the children got older they each had a special part of running the ranch. They raised grade-beef cattle, hay crops, and in later years were known for their spud crops.

Part of the ranch is still owned by the family, and until 2012, they were still producing hay. Now the land is being used as pasture for the family's small cattle herd.

Mayonnaise

Makes 1 cup

JESSIE MILLER
BRUNEAU, IDAHO

1 egg
1 cup vegetable oil
1/2 teaspoon vinegar
1/2 teaspoon lemon juice
1/2 teaspoon salt

With the blade in your food processor, process egg and about 1 tablespoon oil until combined. In a few seconds, add vinegar, lemon juice, and salt. While machine is running, pour remaining oil through the feed tube in a slow steady stream. The longer the processor runs, the thicker the mayonnaise.

Homemade Mayonnaise

Makes 3–3 1/2 cups

BONNIE GASPARD
MAURICE, LOUISIANA

2/3 cup Egg Beaters egg substitute
1 1/2 teaspoons salt
1 teaspoon dried mustard
1 teaspoon sugar
1/2 teaspoon paprika
5 tablespoons vinegar
2 cups canola oil
Black pepper, optional

Combine egg substitute, salt, mustard, sugar, paprika, vinegar, and 1/2 cup oil in blender. Blend on medium-high speed, just until mixed. Without turning off blender, pour in the rest of the oil in a slow steady stream. If necessary, use a rubber spatula to keep the mixture flowing to the blades. Continue blending until the oil is completely incorporated and the mixture is smooth and thick. Add more vinegar for a tangy taste. Add a speck of pepper, if desired.

BAR 11 RANCH
LEADORE, IDAHO

We ranched in Yaak, Montana, before moving to Idaho to ranch. We relocated due to a subdivision forcing us to sell the family ranch. We have ranched here for 20 years and run about 200 mother cows all on deeded land.

Homemade Summer Sausage

Makes 4 rolls

GLENDA MCCONNELL
BAR 11 RANCH
LEADORE, IDAHO

I use this recipe when we have a lot ground beef.

    2 pounds ground beef
    1 cup water
    1/2 teaspoon liquid smoke
    1/2 teaspoon minced onion
    1/2 teaspoon coarsely ground black pepper
    1/2 teaspoon garlic powder
    1/2 teaspoon mustard seeds
    2 tablespoons quick curing salt
       (Morton's Tender Quick salt)

Mix together all ingredients in a nonmetal bowl. It is easier to mix the seasonings with the water then incorporate the meat, using your hands to evenly distribute all the spices. Do not over mix or the meat will be tough. Cover and refrigerate for 24 hours.
Preheat oven to 325 degrees.
Remove mixture from bowl and roll into 4 rolls, about 1 1/2 to 2 inches thick. Wrap in aluminum foil with shiny side towards meat. Punch tiny holes along one side and place on a broiler pan with holes down to drain out liquid. Bake for 1 1/2 hours. Let cool. Remove foil and rewrap in plastic wrap and refrigerate.

Liver Sausage

Serves 4–6

AMBER JOHNS
ELKO, NEVADA

This is an old recipe belonging to my great-grandmother. My great-grandparents homesteaded a ranch in Gardner, Colorado.

2/3 cup ground beef head meat
   (use the fatter part of the head)
1/3 cup ground cooked liver
1 cup minced onion
Salt and pepper, to taste

Have your head meat cooked and reserve cooking liquid. Combine head meat, liver, onion, salt, and pepper. Mix with reserved liquid, working in gradually so it doesn't get too wet. Put to press.

Same-Day Sweet Pickles

Serves 8

ED AND DEANA ALDER
HALE HOMESTEAD
TROUT CREEK, UTAH

- ⅔ cup apple-cider vinegar
- ⅓ cup sugar
- ⅛ teaspoon salt
- 2 cups thinly sliced 'Beit Alpha' cucumbers (about 2 cucumbers)
- 2 red onions, thinly sliced
- 2 tablespoons torn dill sprigs
- 1 teaspoon whole peppercorns
- 3 tablespoons olive oil

In a medium bowl, mix vinegar, sugar, and salt, stirring occasionally, until sugar dissolves. Set aside.

In a nonreactive bowl, combine cucumbers, onions, dill, and peppercorns. Add olive oil to reserved vinegar mixture and stir well. Pour over vegetables and toss to combine. Cover bowl and refrigerate for at least 8 hours before serving. Store pickles, refrigerated, for up to 5 days.

Smothered Okra

BONNIE GASPARD
MAURICE, LOUISIANA

3 pounds chopped onions
1 bushel cut okra
1 pint cooking oil
2 (15-ounce) cans Rotel tomatoes
2 (32-ounce) cans chopped tomatoes
1 (6-ounce) can tomato paste
2 tablespoons Accent flavoring

Combine all ingredients so everything is coated and mixed well and is the desired consistency. Pack in freezer bags and freeze. Heat to serve.

Homemade Laundry Soap

Makes almost 2 gallons or 68 loads*

**PENNI WASDEN
AURORA, UTAH**

      6 cups water
      1/2 cup (or 1/3 bar grated) Fels Naptha bar soap
      1/2 cup Arm & Hammer washing soda (not baking soda)
      1/2 cup 20 Mule Team Borax
      6 1/2 quarts hot water

In a large saucepan, heat 6 cups water. Add grated bar soap and stir until melted. Add washing soda and borax. Stir until dissolved. Remove from heat.

In a 2-gallon bucket, add 6 1/2 quarts hot water and pour soap mixture into water and stir well. Soap will jell after it sits, but it is easy to stir or shake before use.

* Use 1/2 cup per load.

About the Author

Amber Johns grew up on cattle ranches in Colorado, Oregon, and Nevada. Her family is still involved in ranching in Nevada and she is a member of the Elko County CattleWomen. Amber likes recipes that come with a history and credits her mom with her love of a good home-cooked meal. She teaches kindergarten and enjoys spending time with her husband and children.

Photo courtesy of Amber Johns.

Index

Almond Chocolate Bar Cake, Toasted, 135
Amaretto Cake, 126
Appetizer, Easy Ranch, 40
apple:
    Chutney, 160
    Raw Apple Cake, 136
Aunt Mickey's Honey Candy, 151
avocado, in Val's Salsa, 44

bacon:
    Cauliflower Broccoli Salad, 53
    Herb-Crusted Beef Roast, 104
    Johnny Mazetti, 109
Bagged Ice Cream, 155
Banana Pancakes, Chocolate Chip-, 25
Barbara Smith's Chili, 49
barbecue:
    Barbecue Beef Brisket, 84
    Barbecue Beef on a Roll, 89
    Barbecue Beef Roast, 85
    Barbecue Brisket, 86
    Cheesy Barbecue Sloppy Joes, 92
    Easy Quantity Barbecue, 88
Bars, Peach Crumb, 141
beans:
    black:
        Deb's Beefy Pasta Salad, 58
        Easy Beef and Black Bean Chili, 50
        Val's Salsa, 44
    garbanzo, in Deb's Beefy Pasta Salad, 58
    kidney, in Deb's Beefy Pasta Salad, 58
    navy, in Bull-Sale Beans, 72
    Ranch-Style beans, in Mexican Casserole, 114
beef:
    brisket:
        Barbecue Beef Brisket, 84
        Barbecue Brisket, 86
        Dutch Oven Beef Brisket, 102
    canned, in Rex's Recipe—Beef and Rice, 97
    ground:
        Barbara Smith's Chili, 49
        Barbecue Meatballs, 91
        Bull-Sale Beans, 72
        Cheesy Barbecue Sloppy Joes, 92
        Easy Quantity Barbecue, 88
        Grandma Hammond's Casserole, 103
        Homemade Summer Sausage, 165
        Johnny Mazetti, 109
        Meatballs for a Crowd, 112
        Meatloaf or Meatballs and Gravy, 110
        Mexican Casserole, 114
    head meat, in Liver Sausage, 166
    roast:
        Barbecue Beef on a Roll, 89
        Barbecue Beef Roast, 85
        Beef Stroganoff, 98
        Crock-Pot Beef Eye of Round, 100
        Easy Beef and Black Bean Chili, 50
        Herb-Crusted Beef Roast, 104
        Herbed Roasted Beef in Salt Crust, 106
        No-Fail Beef Roast, 115
        Poor Boys Shredded Beef, 116
        Roast Beef Roll-ups, 119
    steak:
        Bonnie's Beef Pepper Steak, 124
        Creamy Crock-Pot Steak, 94
        Crock-Pot Smothered Steak, 101
        Steak from the Grill, 120
    stew meat, in Good Brown Stew, 47
    tri-tip, in Deb's Beefy Pasta Salad, 58
Beef Stroganoff, 98
Beignets, 156
Bill's Coffee Cake, 17
Bonnie's Beef Pepper Steak, 124
bread:
    Coconut Zucchini Bread, 28
    French Bread, 29
    Homemade Bread, 30
    Mexican Cornbread, 32
Breakfast Casserole, 18
Brittle, Peanut, 152
broccoli:
    Cauliflower Broccoli Salad, 53
    Deb's Beefy Pasta Salad, 58
Bull-Sale Beans, 72
Butter, to Make, 158
buttermilk, in Orange Jell-O Salad, 64

cabbage, in Coleslaw, 55
cake:
    Amaretto Cake, 126
    Bill's Coffee Cake, 17
    Chocolate Zucchini Cake, 127
    Grandma Wolf's Whipped Cream Chocolate Cake, 129
    Great-Grandmother's Nut Cake, 130
    Hot-Water Chocolate Cake, 132
    Poor Man's Cake, 133
    Raw Apple Cake, 136
    Rhubarb Cake, 138
    Toasted Almond Chocolate Bar Cake, 135
Candy, Aunt Mickey's Honey, 151
Caramel Popcorn, 154

carrot:
  Corn and Squash
    Soup, 46
  Deb's Beefy Pasta
    Salad, 58
  Good Brown Stew, 47
  Roast Beef Roll-ups, 119
cashews, in Cauliflower
  Broccoli Salad, 53
casserole:
  Breakfast Casserole, 18
  Corn Casserole, 68
  Grandma Hammond's
    Casserole, 103
  Italian Pasta Casserole, 70
  Mexican Casserole, 114
  Onion Casserole, 69
Cauliflower Broccoli
  Salad, 53
celery:
  Country Pea Salad, 57
  Johnny Mazetti, 109
cheese:
  cheddar:
    Cheesy Barbecue
      Sloppy Joes, 92
    Corn Casserole, 68
    Corn Dip, 39
    Country Pea Salad, 57
    Grandma Hammond's
      Casserole, 103
    Ham and Cheese
      Muffins, 33
    Johnny Mazetti, 109
    Mexican Cornbread, 32
    Onion Casserole, 69
    Pecan Dip, 40
    Roast Beef Roll-ups, 119
    Taco Calzones, 122
  cream:
    Breakfast Casserole, 18
    Chocolate Dessert, 146
    Easy Ranch
      Appetizer, 40
    Grandma Hammond's
      Casserole, 103
    Oven-Baked French
      Toast, 22
    Roast Beef Roll-ups, 119
    Toasted Almond
      Chocolate Bar
      Cake, 135
  feta, in Deb's Beefy
    Pasta Salad, 58
  longhorn:
    Julie's Potatoes, 76
    Mexican Casserole, 114

Monterey Jack, in
  Easy Beef and Black
  Bean Chili, 50
mozzarella:
  Italian Pasta
    Casserole, 70
  Surprise Meatballs, 42
Parmesan:
  Alice Goicoechea's
    Garlic Spaghetti, 71
  Cowboy Potatoes, 75
Parmigiano-Reggiano, in
  Sweet Onion Potatoes
    Au Gratin, 78
Swiss, in Sweet Onion
  Potatoes Au Gratin, 78
Cheesy Barbecue
  Sloppy Joes, 92
Cherry Coke Salad, 62
cherry pie filling, in
  Cherry Coke Salad, 62
chiles:
  Bonnie's Beef Pepper
    Steak, 124
  Breakfast Casserole, 18
  Taco Calzones, 122
Chili, Barbara Smith's, 49
Chili, Easy Beef and
  Black Bean, 50
chili sauce, in Barbecue
  Brisket, 86
chocolate:
  Chocolate Chip-Banana
    Pancakes, 25
  Chocolate Dessert, 146
  Chocolate Zucchini
    Cake, 127
  Cowboy Cookies, 142
  Grandma Wolf's
    Whipped Cream
    Chocolate Cake, 129
  Hedge Hog, 149
  Hot-Water Chocolate
    Cake, 132
  Toasted Almond
    Chocolate Bar
    Cake, 135
Chutney, 160
Cobbler, Quick Fruit, 140
coconut:
  Coconut Custard
    Pie, 139
  Coconut Zucchini
    Bread, 28
  Cowboy Cookies, 142
  Frog-Eye Salad, 60
  Orange Jell-O Salad, 64

Sweet Onion Potatoes
  Au Gratin, 78
coffee, in Raw Apple
  Cake, 136
Coffee Cake, Bill's, 17
Coke:
  Cherry Coke Salad, 62
  Dutch Oven Beef
    Brisket, 102
Coleslaw, 55
Coleslaw, Mom's Simple, 54
contributors:
  Alder, Ed and Deana:
    50, 77, 80, 98, 167
  Anderson, Beth:
    14, 81, 151
  Axtell, Jamie Jo: 55,
    62, 91, 119, 127
  Basanez, Lou: 33, 64
  Broussard, Claudette:
    30, 126, 159
  Broussard, Marcus: 92
  Buzzetti, Rachel: 19,
    34, 57, 101, 103,
    139, 149, 153
  Chesser, Dorothy: 47
  Cockrell, Debra:
    22, 58, 75, 110
  Farek, Elsie W.: 114
  Frederick, Victoria: 92
  Garner, Betty: 49, 135
  Gaspard, Bonnie: 18, 32,
    39, 40, 61, 69, 100, 143,
    150, 156, 164, 168
  Gubler, Julie: 42
  Hart, Brenda: 160
  Ipsen, Mark and
    Becky: 72
  Johns, Amber: 158, 166
  Johnson, Carma: 65
  Johnson, Carol: 70,
    109, 130, 133
  Johnson, Darrell: 102
  Johnson, Ginger:
    26, 45, 155
  Johnson, Kari: 44
  Lee, Bret: 92
  Lohr, Tonya: 116
  Lufkin, Robin:
    53, 112, 141
  Malson, Maggie: 94
  McConnell, Glenda: 165
  Menges, Suzanne: 104
  Miller, Jessie: 68, 78,
    106, 142, 163
  Mosser, Sue: 122

Ostler, Gene and
  Bonnie: 124
Parker, Rachel: 25
Slagowski, Billie Sue:
  29, 132, 138, 140, 152
Slavick, Jackie: 136
Spencer, Sherry:
  28, 86, 89, 154
Sullinger, Joan: 97
Tullis, Dona: 84, 85, 88
Van Norman,
  Gerri: 17, 146
Walkup, SA: 120
Wasden, Penni: 170
Wintch, Barbara: 115
Wolf, Barbara: 76
Wolf, Molly: 20,
  35, 40, 54, 60, 71,
  129, 145, 148
cookies:
  Cowboy Cookies, 142
  Fig Cookies, 143
  Traditional Sugar
    Cookies, 145
corn:
  Corn and Squash
    Soup, 46
  Corn Casserole, 68
  Corn Dip, 39
  Mexican Cornbread, 32
  Val's Salsa, 44
corn muffin mix, in
  Corn Casserole, 68
Cornbread, Mexican, 32
cornflakes, in Julie's
  Potatoes, 76
Country Pea Salad, 57
Cowboy Cookies, 142
Cowboy Potatoes, 75
craisins, in Cauliflower
  Broccoli Salad, 53
Cream Puffs, 148
Creamy Crock-Pot Steak, 94
Crock-Pot:
  Creamy Crock-
    Pot Steak, 94
  Crock-Pot Beef Eye
    of Round, 100
  Crock-Pot Smothered
    Steak, 101
cucumber:
  Macaroni Salad, 61
  Same-Day Sweet
    Pickles, 167
Custard Pie, Coconut, 139

Deb's Beefy Pasta Salad, 58

Dip, Corn, 39
Dip, Pecan, 40
Dutch Oven Beef
  Brisket, 102

Easy Beef and Black
  Bean Chili, 50
Easy Quantity Barbecue, 88
Easy Ranch Appetizer, 40
Eggs 'n' Hamburger
  Breakfast, Pancakes and, 20
enchilada sauce, in
  Johnny Mazetti, 109

Fig Cookies, 143
French Bread, 29
French Toast, Oven-
  Baked, 22
Frog-Eye Salad, 60

German Pancakes, 19
Good Brown Stew, 47
Good Popcorn, 153
Grandma Hammond's
  Casserole, 103
Grandma Wolf's
  Whipped Cream
  Chocolate Cake, 129
Great-Grandmother's
  Nut Cake, 130

Ham and Cheese Muffins, 33
Hamburger Breakfast,
  Pancakes and Eggs 'n', 20
Hedge Hog, 149
Herb-Crusted Beef Roast, 104
Herbed Roasted Beef
  in Salt Crust, 106
homemade:
  Homemade Bread, 30
  Homemade Laundry
    Soap, 170
  Homemade
    Mayonnaise, 164
  Homemade Summer
    Sausage, 165
Honey Candy, Aunt
  Mickey's, 151
Hotcakes, Sourdough, 14
Hot-Water Chocolate
  Cake, 132

Ice Cream, Bagged, 155
Italian Pasta Casserole, 70

Jell-O:
  Cherry Coke Salad, 62
  Orange Jell-O Salad, 64

Orange-Tapioca
  Jell-O Salad, 65
Johnny Mazetti, 109
Julie's Potatoes, 76

Laundry Soap,
  Homemade, 170
lettuce, in Roast Beef
  Roll-ups, 119
Lighthouse Ranch
  Dressing: in Mom's
  Simple Coleslaw, 54
Liver Sausage, 166

Macaroni Salad, 61
Mandarin oranges:
  Frog-Eye Salad, 60
  Orange-Tapioca
    Jell-O Salad, 65
Manwich, in Easy
  Quantity Barbecue, 88
Marinade, Steak, 159
marinara sauce, in Italian
  Pasta Casserole, 70
marshmallows:
  Frog-Eye Salad, 60
  Good Popcorn, 153
Mayonnaise, 163
Mayonnaise,
  Homemade, 164
meatballs:
  Barbecue Meatballs, 91
  Meatballs for a
    Crowd, 112
  Meatloaf or Meatballs
    and Gravy, 110
  Surprise Meatballs, 42
Meatloaf or Meatballs
  and Gravy, 110
Mexican Casserole, 114
Mexican Cornbread, 32
Mom's Simple Coleslaw, 54
Morton's Coarse Kosher
  Salt, in Herbed Roasted
  Beef in Salt Crust, 106
muffins:
  Ham and Cheese
    Muffins, 33
  Peach Muffins, 34
  Pumpkin Muffins, 35
mushroom:
  Beef Stroganoff, 98
  Bonnie's Beef Pepper
    Steak, 124
  Johnny Mazetti, 109

No-Fail Beef Roast, 115

noodles, see pasta
Nut Cake, Great-
  Grandmother's, 130
nuts, of choice:
  Bill's Coffee Cake, 17
  Chocolate Dessert, 146
  Coconut Zucchini
    Bread, 28
  Fig Cookies, 143
  Poor Man's Cake, 133

oatmeal:
  Barbecue Meatballs, 91
  Cowboy Cookies, 142
  Meatballs for a
    Crowd, 112
Okra, Smothered, 168
olives, black:
  Deb's Beefy Pasta Salad, 58
  Johnny Mazetti, 109
Onion Casserole, 69
Onion Potatoes Au Gratin,
  Sweet, 78
Orange Jell-O Salad, 64
Orange-Tapioca
  Jell-O Salad, 65
Oven-Baked French Toast, 22

pancakes:
  Chocolate Chip-Banana
    Pancakes, 25
  German Pancakes, 19
  Pancakes and Eggs
    'n' Hamburger
    Breakfast, 20
  Sourdough Hotcakes, 14
pasta and noodles:
  Alice Goicoechea's
    Garlic Spaghetti, 71
  Deb's Beefy Pasta Salad, 58
  Frog-Eye Salad, 60
  Grandma Hammond's
    Casserole, 103
  Italian Pasta Casserole, 70
  Johnny Mazetti, 109
  Macaroni Salad, 61
peach:
  Peach Crumb Bars, 141
  Peach Muffins, 34
Peanut Brittle, 152
Pea Salad, Country, 57
pecans:
  Amaretto Cake, 126
  Cowboy Cookies, 142
  Orange Jell-O Salad, 64
  Peach Muffins, 34
  Pecan Dip, 40

Sweet Onion Potatoes
  Au Gratin, 78
Waverly Pecan Treats, 150
Pecan Dip, 40
pepper:
  bell:
    Barbara Smith's
      Chili, 49
    Bonnie's Beef Pepper
      Steak, 124
    Bull-Sale Beans, 72
    Coleslaw, 55
    Corn and Squash
      Soup, 46
    Creamy Crock-
      Pot Steak, 94
    Ham and Cheese
      Muffins, 33
    Johnny Mazetti, 109
    Macaroni Salad, 61
  jalapeño:
    Corn Dip, 39
    Mexican Cornbread, 32
pepper jelly:
  Easy Ranch Appetizer, 40
  Pecan Dip, 40
pickle relish, in Easy
  Quantity Barbecue, 88
Pickles, Same-Day Sweet, 167
Pie, Coconut Custard, 139
pineapple:
  Cherry Coke Salad, 62
  Frog-Eye Salad, 60
  Orange Jell-O Salad, 64
Poor Man's Cake, 133
popcorn:
  Caramel Popcorn, 154
  Good Popcorn, 153
potato:
  Cowboy Potatoes, 75
  Good Brown Stew, 47
  Julie's Potatoes, 76
  Roasted Baby Potatoes
    with Herbs, 77
  Sweet Onion Potatoes
    Au Gratin, 78
potato chips, in Onion
  Casserole, 69
Pudding, Yorkshire, 81
Pumpkin Muffins, 35

Quick Fruit Cobbler, 140

raisins, in Poor Man's
  Cake, 133
Raw Apple Cake, 136
Rex's Recipe—Beef
  and Rice, 97

Rhubarb Cake, 138
rice:
  Bonnie's Beef Pepper
    Steak, 124
  Creamy Crock-
    Pot Steak, 94
  Rex's Recipe—Beef
    and Rice, 97
Roast Beef Roll-ups, 119
Roasted Baby Potatoes
  with Herbs, 77
Roll-ups, Roast Beef, 119

salad:
  Cauliflower Broccoli
    Salad, 53
  Cherry Coke Salad, 62
  Country Pea Salad, 57
  Deb's Beefy Pasta
    Salad, 58
  Frog-Eye Salad, 60
  Macaroni Salad, 61
  Orange Jell-O Salad, 64
  Orange-Tapioca
    Jell-O Salad, 65
Same-Day Sweet Pickles, 167
sausage:
  Breakfast Casserole, 18
  Bull-Sale Beans, 72
  Homemade Summer
    Sausage, 165
  Liver Sausage, 166
  Meatloaf or Meatballs
    and Gravy, 110
  Mexican Cornbread, 32
Shredded Beef, Poor
  Boys, 116
Sloppy Joes, Cheesy
  Barbecue, 92
Smothered Okra, 168
Smothered Steak,
  Crock-Pot, 101
Soap, Homemade
  Laundry, 170
soup:
  canned:
    condensed beef
      broth, in Beef
      Stroganoff, 98
    condensed cream
      of chicken:
        Julie's Potatoes, 76
        Mexican
          Casserole, 114
    condensed cream
      of mushroom:
        Creamy Crock-
          Pot Steak, 94

Meatloaf or Meatballs and Gravy, 110
Onion Casserole, 69
condensed tomato:
   Crock-Pot Smothered Steak, 101
   Easy Quantity Barbecue, 88
   Johnny Mazetti, 109
onion soup mix:
   Dutch Oven Beef Brisket, 102
   Easy Quantity Barbecue, 88
Soup, Corn and Squash, 46
sour cream:
   Amaretto Cake, 126
   Beef Stroganoff, 98
   Corn Casserole, 68
   Corn Dip, 39
   Grandma Hammond's Casserole, 103
   Grandma Wolf's Whipped Cream Chocolate Cake, 129
   Julie's Potatoes, 76
   Rhubarb Cake, 138
Sourdough Hotcakes, 14
sourdough rolls, in Barbecue Beef on a Roll, 89
soy sauce, in Steak Marinade, 159
Spaghetti, Alice Goicoechea's Garlic, 71
spinach, in Deb's Beefy Pasta Salad, 58
Squash Soup, Corn and, 46
Steak from the Grill, 120

Steak Marinade, 159
Stew, Good Brown, 47
Stroganoff, Beef, 98
Sugar Cookies, Traditional, 145
Summer Sausage, Homemade, 165
sunflower seeds, in Deb's Beefy Pasta Salad, 58
Surprise Meatballs, 42
Sweet Onion Potatoes Au Gratin, 78
Sweet Pickles, Same-Day, 167
sweet potato, in Sweet Onion Potatoes Au Gratin, 78
Sweet Potato Soufflé, 80
Syrup, 22

Taco Calzones, 122
Tapioca Jell-O Salad, Orange-, 65
Texas toast, in Cheesy Barbecue Sloppy Joes, 92
Toasted Almond Chocolate Bar Cake, 135
tomato:
   Barbara Smith's Chili, 49
   Bonnie's Beef Pepper Steak, 124
   Cheesy Barbecue Sloppy Joes, 92
   Chutney, 160
   Corn Dip, 39
   Crock-Pot Smothered Steak, 101
   Easy Beef and Black Bean Chili, 50
   Macaroni Salad, 61
   Mexican Casserole, 114
   Smothered Okra, 168

Val's Salsa, 44
tomato sauce:
   Grandma Hammond's Casserole, 103
   Johnny Mazetti, 109
tortillas:
   Mexican Casserole, 114
   Roast Beef Roll-ups, 119
Traditional Sugar Cookies, 145

Val's Salsa, 44

Waffles, Whole-Wheat, 26
walnuts:
   Great-Grandmother's Nut Cake, 130
   Raw Apple Cake, 136
Waverly crackers, in Waverly Pecan Treats, 150
Waverly Pecan Treats, 150
Whipped Cream Chocolate Cake, Grandma Wolf's, 129
whipped topping:
   Chocolate Dessert, 146
   Frog-Eye Salad, 60
   Orange Jell-O Salad, 64
   Orange-Tapioca Jell-O Salad, 65
   Toasted Almond Chocolate Bar Cake, 135
white wine, in Beef Stroganoff, 98
Whole-Wheat Waffles, 26

Yorkshire Pudding, 81

zucchini:
   Chocolate Zucchini Cake, 127
   Coconut Zucchini Bread, 28

Metric Conversion Chart

Volume Measurements		Weight Measurements		Temperature Conversion	
U.S.	Metric	U.S.	Metric	Fahrenheit	Celsius
1 teaspoon	5 ml	1/2 ounce	15 g	250	120
1 tablespoon	15 ml	1 ounce	30 g	300	150
1/4 cup	60 ml	3 ounces	90 g	325	160
1/3 cup	75 ml	4 ounces	115 g	350	180
1/2 cup	125 ml	8 ounces	225 g	375	190
2/3 cup	150 ml	12 ounces	350 g	400	200
3/4 cup	175 ml	1 pound	450 g	425	220
1 cup	250 ml	2 1/4 pounds	1 kg	450	230